A New Approach to
The Tao Te Ching

by **Jerry O. Dalton**

HUMANICS NEW AGE

Atlanta, Georgia

Humanics New Age
P.O. Box 7400
Atlanta, Georgia 30309

Humanics New Age is an imprint of Humanics Limited.

First Printing - 1994

Many illustrations are from *The Mustard Seed Garden Manual of Painting* translated from the Chinese and edited by Mai-mai Sze, Bollington Series, Princeton University Press, New York, 1956. These illustrations, originally reproduced by wood block printing, were created in the seventeenth century by three brothers: Wang Kei, Wang Shih, and Wang Nieh.

PRINTED IN THE UNITED STATES OF AMERICA

Library of Congress Cataloging in Publication Data
Dalton, Jerry O.
            Tao Te Ching: backward down the path / Jerry o. Dalton.
                    p.   cm.
            Includes bibliographical references.
            ISBN 0-89334-223-8 : $14.95
            1. Lao-tzu. Tao te ching   I. Lao-tzu.   Tao te ching. 1993.
        II. Title.
        BL1900.l35d35   1993
        299'.51482--dc20   93-1946
                                                                    CIP

Dedicated to:

my wife, Judy

my children, Christie and Dan

and my brother, C.G.

Acknowledgements

Thanks to the more than thirty Taoist sages whose works are listed in Appendix 1. Each of these people have looked into their hearts and rendered the timeless wisdom of the Tao Te Ching in their own terms. Each and every one of them has helped me to understand as much as I do. For that priceless gift of understanding I am profoundly grateful.

Table of Contents

Key to Pronunciation

Lao is pronounced as if it rhymes with how.
Tzu is pronounced as ds sounds in the word adds.
Tao is pronounced dow and rhymes with how.
Te is pronounced as du sounds in the word duck.
Ching is pronounced jing as in the word jingle

Preface

One of the most difficult questions about the Tao Te Ching is why it has such lasting interest. The answer, like the Tao, has components relating to both the inner subtleties and the outer manifestations.

In the West there is a strong tendency to cleave things apart and to place the pieces in neat glass-covered compartments for study and analysis. This tendency has extended even into the unseen subtleties of metaphysics, religion, and psychology and has resulted in a vague malaise and sense of wrongness about our lives.

An overview of the differences between Eastern and Western religious thought casts some light on the source of this wrongness. Joseph Campbell, in his book The Masks of God: Oriental Mythology, sharply delineates the fundamental religious configurations of East and West. I had understood that in the West there was a separation between mankind and an anthropomorphic God, while in the East there was an inward-directed search for reunion with the Mystical Oneness, that is, a return to the great origin. But, as Campbell points out, Western religion aims at determining man's relationship to a distinct, transcendent God who is forever separate from mankind. The separation exists from the creation forward and leads to a view of creation, Adam's fall from grace, and all religious happenings since, as historical and ethical events. Campbell says that Eastern religion centers on the view that creation was the fragmentation of oneness as personified in God, and that the divine is therefore inherent in eveything. In the East salvation comes through a casting aside of illusions and ignorance caused by ego, and by the recognizing and reintegrating with the divine oneness found within. In the West a historical event - Adam's fall - separated us from the grace of a separate God and only a historical event - the end of time - will bring us back into grace with a still separate God. In the East reunification with the fragmented divine oneness requires only self-examination and an altering of our psychological orientation. The Western view is historical, ethical, and externally directed toward another life in another realm. The Eastern view is metaphysical, poetic, and internally directed toward a correct and egoless life in this realm.

In the West the separation of mankind from God requires that both have a domain, a holy city and a secular city. For us to achieve grace and to return to the holy city some part of us must be able to survive physical death and earthly discorporation. So Descartes wielded the logical cleaver and said "I think therefore I am", and the spirit was neatly separated from the body. This separation instills many practitioners of Western religion with a drive for the after-life in heaven and an almost casual disregard for the manifestations of the secular, corporeal world. It gives a zealous incentive to conquer profane nature rather than to participate in its sacred but not divine unity.

On a psychological plane, as opposed to metaphysical, Descartes split the brain and its function into the logical, pragmatic, empirical, left-brainedness of the masculine West and the intuitive, poetic, artistic, right-brainedness of the feminine East. This gave Westerners a science that could and would dissect anything into its component parts in the interest of logical understanding. It also gave us a technology based in that understanding, capable of amazingly complex fabrications and manipulations on the one hand, and of a resulting devastating destruction of nature on the other. But, because our religion told us that we were only temporary residents, we used science and technology to help us in the conquest of the profane. We forgot that we were charged with stewardship by that same religion.

We have only just begun to realize that the religious and psychological configurations, that were going to save us from immersion in the physical world and propel us to heaven, have instead made us vandals who have sacked and desecrated the very temple in which we must live.

It is this sense of wrongness of the path which we collectively pursue which has turned my attention to the wandering Taoist sage. He participates in and finds accord with nature and the natural way of heaven and earth. This book is the manifestation of my efforts to understand Taoism, and to present it for others to consider. I am driven by the conviction that if enough people were to read and understand the Tao Te Ching, the world would be profoundly influenced and thereby improved. This work is presented in the enduring hope that it will help others, as it has helped me, to turn away from the path we are pursuing. It is not too late to retrace the false steps which have brought us to this point. It is not too late to turn and begin a healing journey - backward down the path.

How To Approach The Tao Te Ching

A few words are required about the organization, content, and use of this book.

Interpretation:

The first part of each chapter is an interpretation of the Tao Te Ching which was synthesized from the study of the thirty some-odd translations and interpretations listed in Appendix 1. My interpretation is as technically correct as I could make it through study of the works of the many who had gone before. In order to make the Tao Te Ching more accessible to a logical approach I have broken each chapter into numbered sections, each of which consists of a single thought. The divisions which I have made correspond for the most part to paragraph divisions made in many of the texts which I have studied.

Paraphrase:

The Tao Te Ching is enigmatic in part as any discussion of the mystical and transcendental must be. It is also wildly practical in its straight-forward advice to those who would lead themselves as well as others. Its description of the sage or ideal person shows us how to seek internal wisdom and outward leadership. Its lessons are tied to simple examples from nature which serve both to illustrate and to remind us all that we are part of nature and not separate from it. I have written a paraphrase of each chapter in order to present the lessons of the Tao Te Ching in simple, modern, and understandable terms.

For Thought:

Our existence as human beings is divided into our inner psychological and spiritual life, and our outer life of action and interaction with people and things around us. I have included a For Thought section with each chapter which addresses the inner life. It is designed to make one think about how the lessons of the chapter relate both to the individual and to the world. The reader is encouraged to look behind the superficialities of life and to examine what he or she finds there in the light of the non-conventional wisdom of the Tao Te Ching.

For Action:

The For Action sections illustrate the applicability of the lessons of the Tao Te Ching to every-day personal behavior and situations. In them are simple concrete things which can be done as manifestations of the practice of Taoism or which expand one's understanding of Taoism. The reader is encouraged to act both logically and intuitively depending on the situation. Above all, the aim is to make the reader realize that Taoism is a working philosophy and that knowing Tao is not being Tao.

Related Reading:

The Tao Te Ching a non-linear work. By non-linearity I mean that the book does not begin at chapter one and progress in logical lock-step to chapter eighty-one where loose ends are tucked in and conclusions are drawn. One cannot pick up the Tao Te Ching, turn to the last chapter, and discover how it turns out. I have included a Related Reading section at the end of each chapter which lists specific chapters or sections with thoughts related to the one at hand. This list will allow the student of the Tao Te Ching to trace individual threads of thought through the whole tapestry of the work.

Approaches:

From the onset of this work I have hoped that it would serve as a practical guide to the mystical and a mystical guide to the practical. There can be many approaches to the study and use of the Tao Te Ching. The reader should choose the one most suited to his or her needs.

Logical and Linear:

Start at Chapter 1 and read through to the end. Read the Paraphrase of each chapter for an interpretation in more modern vernacular and context. Use the Related Reading section to find related chapters and sections.

Personal Application:

Review the chapter titles in the Table of Contents. Pick one or more chapters that seem to be of interest or applicable to your situation. The For Thought and For Action sections of each chapter may be of particular utility in this approach.

Intuitive and Synchronistic:

Simply open the book and read the chapter before you. Alternatively you might read the book in the same manner in which I wrote it. Make eighty-one numbered slips of paper and place them in a bowl. Each time you want to read the Tao Te Ching draw out a slip and read the chapter whose number appears.

In all three cases you may want to keep a journal with notes on your reading and as a record of your application and understanding. You might also see how many translations and interpretations you can find so that you can see the different viewpoints of the many people who have studied the Tao Te Ching before you. Appendix 1 has a chronological listing of the translations which I have acquired in the last few years. Many of these are readily available in any good bookstore. There are also many fine books on Taoism available as additional aids to study and understanding. A few are listed in Appendix 2.

THE TRANSCENDENTAL TAO

1:1 The Tao of words is not the transcendental Tao.
The spoken name is not the transcendental name.

1:2 The nameless is the beginning of all things.
The named is the mother of all things.

1:3 Constantly desireless, one can see the subtlety;
Constantly desiring, one can only see the manifestations.
These two are the same but differ in name.
The mystery is in the unity.
Where the mystery is most profound is the gateway to all mystery.

Paraphrase:
1:1 Something about which we can know nothing existed before time and space. Call it Tao. But recognize that we cannot correctly name it. Names define and limit. The something which we will call Tao is undefined and limitless.

1:2 This something was the origin of the universe and its workings. Once it showed itself as the physical universe, through natural process, it became everything in the universe. Thus it is the mother of all things.

1:3 It is only by removing all desire and blanking the mind that we can participate in the mystical subtlety of Tao. With a desire for knowledge we can see and understand the manifestations of Tao. These two approaches differ, in that the first is intuitive and mystical, while the second is logical and rational. Though they differ in name, either approach works because ultimately they are the same. Recognizing this unity is an intuitive insight into the nature of Tao. Accumulation of such insights leads to a profound, mystical understanding and oneness with Tao.

For Thought:
In the Western world we are trained from an early age to use rational, logical, linear thought. We are encouraged to discount the value of intuition. The key to understanding Tao is to discard expectations and preconceived notions about logic and intuition. Recognize that intuitive understanding may be the result of your unconscious and illogical mind assimilating and organizing information in ways that your conscious and logical mind cannot.

For Action:
Think back through your experience. Identify times when you just knew that an answer to a problem or resolution of a situation was right. Write down one instance which seems especially significant along with your recollection of the actual outcome of your intuition. Remember that neither intuition nor logic are right one hundred percent of the time. The key is in using both left-brain logic and right-brain intuition to achieve a balanced approach to life.

Related Reading:
Section 1:1 Read 25 (all)
Section 1:2 Read 4 (all), 14 (all)
Section 1:3 Read 21 (all), 40:2, 42:1

RECOGNIZING DUALITIES

2:1   When all people know beauty as beauty, ugliness arises.
       When all people know good as good, evil arises.
       Thus being and non-being generate each other.
       Difficult and easy complement each other.
       Long and short form each other.
       High and low support each other.
       Tone and voice harmonize each other.
       Front and back follow each other.

2:2   Therefore the sage:
       Manages affairs without action,
       Teaches without speech,
       All things arise but he doesn't originate them.
       He works without expectation,
       Accomplishes without taking credit.
       Because he takes no credit,
       The credit remains with him.

Paraphrase:
2:1   By defining a concept we define its opposite. Thus the original duality of being and non-being is mirrored in the dualities of the physical world. If one thing is difficult, there must be something else which is easy by comparison. The same is true for long and short, high and low, and so on.

2:2   Sages practice action without deeds. They teach by example. Natural processes go on around them, but sages do not start them. They work without dwelling on rewards or noteriety. They accomplish results without trumpeting their own achievements. Because they demand no credit, people are happy to give them credit.

For Thought:
One of the keys to Taoist thought is the recognition of dualities. All processes have active and passive principles. All physical conditions have opposites. Most failures come from thinking of the dualities as polarities. Instead of seeing active and passive aspects of action as complementary, we label one as good, automatically making the other bad, and try to ignore or eliminate the other. This makes no more sense than trying to cut a magnet in two to remove one of the poles.

For Action:
Pick a personal or business situation in which you can control the flow of events, either by your own actions or by directing the actions of others. Before you act or direct others to do so, look closely at the process which is unfolding. Identify the action which you can initiate that will encounter the least reaction or resistance from others, while forwarding your goals the most. Don't forget to consider whether things will go the way you want if you do nothing.

Related Reading:
Section 2:1   Read 40:2
Section 2:2   Read 29:1, 43:2, 47 (all), 48 (all), 57:3, 63:1

ABANDONING DESIRES AND STRATEGY   *3.*

3:1   Do not exalt the worthy,
        To avoid contention.
        Do not treasure rare goods,
        To avoid thievery.
        Do not display desirable things,
        To avoid discontent.

3:2   Therefore the sage leads others by;
        Emptying their minds,
        Stuffing their bellies,
        Diluting their ambition,
        Concentrating their strength.

3:3   If the people are without strategy or desire,
        And the clever are afraid to interfere,
        Then order will prevail.

Paraphrase:
3:1   Holding one person up as an example for others will cause jealousy and con-
tention. If you attach great value to material goods, then people will try to steal them. If
you advertise material things as being highly desirable, then people will lose their focus.

3:2   Sages recognize these truths. So they lead others by emptying their minds of
superficial and artificial desires. They attend to the natural, basic needs of people. They
weaken ego-serving ambition. They increase the natural potency and power of people.

3:3   When people act without self-serving strategy or desire for gain and do not use
cleverness to interfere with the natural flow of process, order will prevail.

For Thought:
Many things which we are conditioned to believe are important are superficial. For example, a car is a means of transportation. There are speed limits. Why are cars made to go
so much faster? Petroleum is a non-renewable natural resource. Thus, a small, energy
efficient engine is desirable. Why do we see commercials showing powerful vehicles
speeding around curves and down country lanes? What is there about an inanimate
object with no human characteristics that possibly can be sexy? None of these questions
relate to the fundamental function of an automobile. Why are cars presented this way?

For Action:
For one whole day evaluate all commercials and ads you see as if you were an alien
totally new to the planet. Do political ads present real solutions to real issues? Do talk
show commercials promise to inform and educate you? Do you really have to smell,
dress, or look a certain way to be a productive member of society? After you have sorted
through your thoughts, ask how your life might be changed if you evaluated everything
this way and responded only to the real and not the superficial.

Related Reading:
Section 3:1   Read 12:1, 13 (all), 29:3, 38:3, 44:1, 46:2, 64:5
Section 3:2   Read 12:2, 15:2, 49:3, 65:1
Section 3:3   Read 19:1, 48:2, 57:3, 58 (all)

THE NATURE OF TAO

4:1   The Tao is an empty vessel, yet its use is inexhaustible.
        It is the profound source of all things.

4:2   It blunts the sharpness,
        Untangles the knots,
        Mutes the glare,
        Combines with dust.

4:3   It is pure, still, and ever present,
        I do not know its origin.
        Its image precedes the lord.

Paraphrase:
4:1   The Tao is a vessel which is both the source and receptacle for all things. It simultaneously empties and fills. It can never be exhausted.

4:2   Within the greater context of the Tao all things are levelled, blunted, muted, and simplified.

4:3   The Tao is unlimited in creative power. It is everywhere and always.

For Thought:
Tao is a word which can be both a noun and a verb. It conveys both the idea of a path and the act of walking on a path. This chapter calls attention to the nature of Tao by asking us to see it as an inexhaustible vessel which produces things from no-thingness. It is both the form of the vessel and the function of producing things from the vessel.

For Action:
To get an idea of the difficulty of presenting this concept, think about what may have existed before anything existed. Write down your thoughts in a few sentences. Do you know what omnificent means? Look it up.

Related Reading:
Section 4:1   Read 5:2, 6 (all), 35:2, 45:1
Section 4:2   Read 56:2

DISINTERESTED INTEREST

5:1   The universe is impartial.
        It regards all things as straw dogs.
        The sage is impartial.
        He regards people as straw dogs.

5:2   The universe is like a bellows.
        It is empty but never exhausted.
        The more it moves the more it yields.

5:3   Too many words are exhausting.
        Better to hold to the center.

Paraphrase:
5:1   Nature is impartial and plays no favorites. So are sages.

5:2   Nature is like a bellows. It is both empty and an inexhaustible source. The moving of the Tao process in nature continually yields more.

5:3   The more words we use to explain this unexplainable process, the more exhausted we become. It is better to go inward to the core of your being and intuitively understand what cannot be logically explained.

For Thought:
The literal translation of this chapter carries negative connotations for the Western reader, thus some clarification is necessary. The word impartial means unbiased rather than indifferent. Straw dogs is a reference to the Chinese practice of using dogs fashioned of straw in religious rites. Before and during the ceremony the dogs were treated with deference as if they had great value. When the rite was completed the dogs were cast aside and swept up to be used as fuel for fires.

For Action:
This chapter carries practical instructions for personal conduct and interactions. The three critical points are as follows:
(1) Conduct yourself with impartiality. Observe and participate in life with disinterested interest. This course of action will eliminate self-serving, selfish interest from your conduct and interactions. It will enable you to see more clearly such motives in others. Awareness of underlying process will help you to discharge and depolarize conflicts and to proceed with a natural, productive process. It will fulfill your natural power and potentiality.
(2) Detach yourself from empty rites and hollow symbols. Excessive emotional attachment to rites and symbols causes misdirection and ignorance. Remember that rites and symbols are tools for recognizing and tapping the reality of underlying process. When they lose their efficacy as tools, they are broken and should be put aside like the straw dogs of ancient China.
(3) Discard and disregard intellectualizations, rationalizations, and sophistry. Spend time each day seeking out the center of your being. Hold on to this natural core of values, racial memory, and intuitive knowledge. It is the source of your power and the origin of your potentiality.

Related Reading:
Section 5:1   Read 32:1, 38:3, 56:3, 79:3
Section 5:2   Read 4:1, 6 (all), 11 (all), 35:2
Section 5:3   Read 12:2, 52:2, 56:2

9

THE MYSTIC FEMALE

6:1   The valley spirit never dies.
      It is called the mystic female.
      The gateway of the mystic female,
      Is called the root of the universe.
      Barely visible like a veil,
      Use it, it will never fail.

Parapharase:
6:1   The yin principle is eternal. It is the mystic feminine principle. All things were born out of this principle. It is the generative principle of a nascent Tao. It underlies all things and so is difficult to discern. Those who tap its power find that it is never used up.

For Thought:
This chapter is quoted in another old Chinese text and is attributed to the legendary Yellow Emporer of the Third Millenium B.C. If this is true, then Taoism was carried as a verbal tradition for at least two thousand years before it was set down in writing in the Tao Te Ching.

For Action:
Read the following passage until you can remember all the images, not necessarily the words, in proper sequence. Then relax, close your eyes and travel the path in your mind. Repeat this as often as you wish. With each repetition try to see sharper images in your mind's eye.

You are standing on the south side of a valley. It is a cool evening and to your left a full moon shines down with a brilliant liquid light. There are silver highlights on the foliage. There is a path at your feet. It descends along the steep bluffs which form the valley wall. The bottom of the valley is hidden in mists. From above the mists look like swirling silver-white pools dancing in the moonlight.

Walk down the path. It hugs the valley wall. It is broad and packed hard by long ages of use. To your right are the stone outcroppings of the cliff. To your left the ground falls away into the valley. Look down and see the tops of dark pines on the valley sides. The mists rise up to meet you as you descend.

The path bends around a large stone outcropping. Beyond it there is the sound of water splashing on rocks. Here the path goes under an overhanging formation. Walk under the stone ledge. You are behind a small waterfall. Look out through the falling stream of drops. They are like falling jewels as they catch the moonlight. The water trickles down among loose rock, then finds a small draw and forms a stream which goes down to disappear into the mists below. The foliage around the stream is lush and heavy. It is sprinkled with cleansing droplets of mist and water which sparkle like sequins.

Continue down the path. The mists swirl around you and bring a profound sense of peace and tranquility. There is a diffuse silvery light. Finally the path broadens and moves away from the valley wall. The ground is level. Here there is a small clear area surrounded by ancient oaks. Their limbs intertwine overhead to form a natural shrine. In the center of the clearing, almost hidden by the white mist, there is a stone with a depression in its middle that forms a natural bench. There is the form of a woman sitting there. Mists swirl about her. She raises her hand and beckons for you to approach.

This place and this feminine figure before you inspires awe and a sense of natural sacredness.

A soft melodious voice says, "I am the mystic female, the valley spirit." She invites you to sit with her and you do. There is a feeling of vast, nurturing serenity and peace. Bask in its glow.

After a while, maybe minutes, maybe hours, you prepare to depart this mystical personage and place. As you come to the edge of the clearing, the voice sounds again saying, "You are my child. Return as often as you need me."

Make your way back up the path. The mists thin, then clear as you approach the waterfall. Now the moon is lower. As you stand under the ledge and look out it seems that the drops leave the edge of the rocks above and wash across the lunar face. They fall like liquid diamonds. Step forward and put your hands out. Feel the water splashing into your hands. It runs down your arms. Feel the warmth of the earth and the luminous power of the moon in the droplets. Rub your hands together. Feel the rejuvenating and cleansing power of the water. Touch your forehead with the water. Feel your mind clear and become as calm as the surface of a moon-lit pool. Linger a while.

Now leave the waterfall and continue up the path. Walk slowly. Sense the spirits of pilgrims who have come this way for many thousands of years. Finally you are near the top of the path. The waning light of the moon reveals these words inscribed in the stone of the valley wall...

> The valley spirit never dies.
> It is called the mystic female.
> The gateway of the mystic female,
> Is called the source of all things.
> Barely visible like a veil,
> Use it, it will never fail.

Now there is a glorious golden dawn. Open your eyes and step into it with renewed vitality. Take strength from the knowledge that the collective spirit of every pilgrim who ever walked this way now walks with you. Take comfort in the knowledge that you can always turn and go backward down the path.

Related Reading:
Section 6:1   Read 4:1, 5:2, 35:2, 45:1, 52:1

Reflections

_____

_____

_____

_____

_____

_____

_____

_____

_____

_____

_____

_____

_____

_____

SELF-EFFACEMENT, SELF-ENHANCEMENT 7.

7:1   The universe is eternal.
            Why is the universe eternal?
            It does not live for itself,
            Thus it is everlasting.

7:2   Therefore the sage takes the hindmost,
            And emerges foremost.
            He effaces himself,
            And is one with all.
            Because he desires nothing,
            He has everything.

Paraphrase:
7:1   The universe endures because it has no self-awareness. By being universal it is everlasting.

7:2   Sages emulate this lack of self-awareness by putting selfish interests aside. Because they are detached from the particular they are one with the universal. They want nothing and have everything.

For Thought:
In a continued recognition of the dynamic balance of dualities, Lao Tzu teaches that to effortlessly go to the fore one need only to strive to be behind. By adopting selfless goals aimed only at enhancing the Tao process, you will find that others recognize your power and efficacy. They will look to you as a leader.

For Action:
Instead of struggling and competing today, consciously seek out a job that no one else wants to do. Do it with enthusiasm. Detach yourself from ideas of self-sacrifice and resentment toward those whom you think should have done the task. When you are finished, think about what you have learned from doing the job.

Related Reading:
Section 7:1   Read 34:1, 50 (all)
Section 7:2   Read 66:2, 67:2

EXCELLENCE AND NON-CONTENTION

8.

8:1   The highest excellence is like water.
        Water excels in benefitting all beings without contending.
        It stays in places that men reject,
        And therefore is close to the Tao.

8:2   The excellence of a dwelling is in its location.
        The excellence of a mind is in its depth.
        The excellence in giving is in being like heaven.
        The excellence in speech is in truth.
        The excellence in leadership is in order.
        The excellence in work is in competence.
        The excellence in action is in timing.

8:3   He who does not contend will be free from blame.

Paraphrase:
8:1   The highest excellence is like water. It does not contend, but flows downward along the path of least resistance. By seeking places that are not valued by self-serving people, water approaches the natural Tao process.

8:2   The excellent dwelling has rightness of location for the dweller. The excellent mind is not superficial, but thinks deeply. The excellent giver gives through benevolence and not self-righteousness. Excellent speech is, first and foremost, truthful. Excellent leadership brings order out of chaos. Excellent work is done with correctness and competence. Excellent action is taken at the proper time.

8:3 The practitioner of excellence finds it unecessary to contend and thus is blameless.

For Thought:
This chapter is a capsule summary of a personal transformation to excellence. In dwelling, establish your roots in the earth. Go deeply into your mind to find ancient truth. Give from the heart, speak the truth, establish order, strive for competence in work, and seek proper timing in all you do. Above all, be flexible and accomodating like water. Non-contention is the key to excellence.

For Action:
Each day touch one or more of the keys to excellence in this chapter. Spend a few minutes in meditation, looking inward. Take actions which cultivate excellence in yourself and others. How can you help to bring order to a chaotic workplace? What truth would help you and others to become more competent? What gift of knowledge, care, or compassion can you give from the heart? Think about these things and, above all, do not contend with yourself or others.

Related Reading:
Section 8:1   Read 66:1, 66:2, 78 (all)
Section 8:2   Read 27:1
Section 8:3   Read 22:2, 66:4, 68:1, 81:3

AVOIDING EXCESS

9:1   Better to stop in time than to overfill a vessel.
        Oversharpen a blade and it will soon lose its edge.
        A store of gold and jade cannot be protected.
        Pride in wealth and rank brings calamity on oneself.
        Withdraw when the work is done.
        This is the Tao of heaven.

Paraphrase:
9:1   Don't overdo it. It is better to stop short, than to fill to the brim. It is better not
to try to be sharper than anyone else. The more riches that you acquire, the more likely
that you will be robbed. The more pride that you have, the more likely that you will be
humiliated. Instead, do a full day's work, then retire without calling attention to yourself. This is the way of Tao.

For Thought:
Nothing is static in nature. Even the greatest mountain range, though enduring, will
eventually weather away. So also are we. There are only two phases in our lives, growth
and decay. The moment we say with pride, "I have arrived," we will fall into decline.

For Action:
Today begin a never-ending cycle of growth toward excellence. Do so with no intention
of fame or wealth. Live each day in fullness. Grow in your work and relationships and
retire quietly when each job is finished. Pattern yourself after the Japanese painter who
painted cranes. Each year he improved in mastery of line and form until, at a ripe old
age, he could create magnificent paintings of cranes with a few simple strokes of the
brush. He was an acknowledged master whose paintings were prized by all. But while on
his death bed he said in so many words, "If I only had a few more years, I would have
gotten really good."

Related Reading:
Section 9:1   Read 15:2, 29:3, 30:2, 55:3

DEVELOPING THROUGH DISCIPLINE

10:1   In embracing the one with body and soul,
        Can you be undivided?
        In controlling your vital breath,
        Can you be supple as a new born child?
        In cleansing your inner vision,
        Can you make it flawless?
        Can you love and lead the people,
        Without cunning?
        In opening and closing the gateway to heaven,
        Can you be like the female?
        In seeing all things clearly,
        Can you be without erudition?

10:2   Bearing and nourishing,
        Bearing without possessing,
        Rearing without ruling,
        This is the mystic virtue.

Paraphrase:
10:1   In the practice of the Tao can you heal the schism between head and heart?
Can you control your life force so that you always remain flexible? Can you love and lead
people without self-serving trickery? In participating in the Tao process can you embrace
the feminine principle? Can you use intuition and discard erudition?

10:2   Mystic potential bears and nourishes without claiming ownership. It rears
without dominating.

For Thought:
Embracing the one with body and soul can be interpreted on both a personal and a cosmological level. At the personal level, it could refer to the reintegration of body and
soul, of left-brain and right brain, and of the feminine and masculine principles that
reside in us all. On a cosmological scale, embracing the one could refer to a journey
backward down the path to the natural simplicity of an infant and beyond to the mystical no-thingness of the original, eternal Tao.

For Action:
Some athletes use a sort of meditation to think themselves through the complex
motions and actions associated with their event. Other people use creative visualization
to imagine themselves accomplishing personal goals and to focus on the actions
required. Close your eyes and visualize yourself walking down a path which leads from a
rocky mountainside down into a lush mist-filled valley. As you go down the path visualize complexities and problems dissolving away in the coolness of the valley. See yourself becoming child-like as you look about in wonder at the thickening, swirling mass.
Notice how the mist hides superficial details of trees and plants so that you can see
only the shapes and essences. Go down the path until the mists are so thick you can see
nothing external. Then look inside yourself and see everything.

Related Reading:
Section 10:1   Read 6 (all), 22:2, 28:1, 39:1, 65:2
Section 10:2   Read 2:2, 51:2

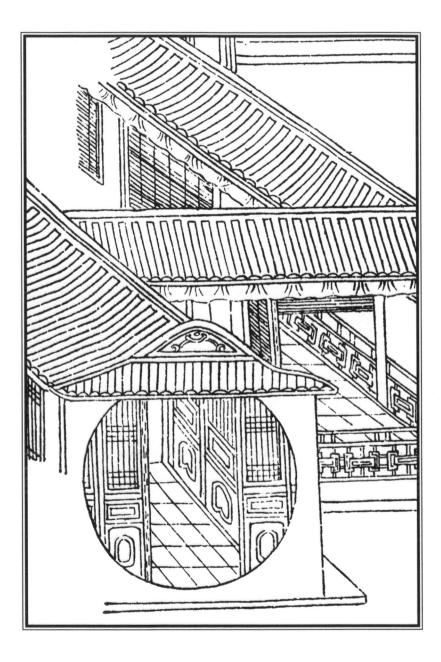

PRACTICAL FORM, USEFUL EMPTINESS 11.

11:1   Thirty spokes share one hub,
The space at the center makes the wheel useful.
Mold clay to form a vessel,
The space within makes it useful.
Cut doors and windows in walls,
The space within makes the room useful.
Therefore, what exists serves for benefit,
What does not exist serves for usefulness.

Paraphrase:
11:1   A wheel has solid form but the hole for the axle is what makes it useful. The same is true for a bowl and for a room. All of these things have a practical form, but the emptiness at the center of each is where the usefulness lies.

For Thought:
We have been trained to manipulate things and to think that such manipulation is the ultimate control. But practical form is not the only reality. Manifestations are only clues to the critical underlying process. Understanding this process leads to true power and development of our potentiality. Yet, this process cannot be seen, felt, smelled, tasted, or heard. It is not measurable, so our senses say that it is not there. It is void, but nonetheless it is real, useful, and central to everything.

For Action:
In searching for the Tao process one must not be misled by either the senses or a cluttered mind. Use the following as a creative visualization or meditation to help you to find Tao process within yourself: Think of your mind as a large attic in your house. It has been accumulating things for the entire time you have lived here and now you want to use it for a studio where you can develop your creative potential. But first you must clean it out. Go into the room and look around you. There are lots of things here which you have stored. They seemed important when you put them here but now they are collecting dust. Is your attic really cluttered? It probably is. Pick up the closest thing at hand. What is it? Why is it here? Is it something someone gave to you that you really didn't want but that you were afraid to refuse for fear of offending them? Is it something that you simply had to have, but once you had it, it seemed to lose its appeal? Look at it, think about it. Will it really be a loss if you discard it or will it be a release instead? Consider this thing carefully and, if it has no value to you, discard it. Go to the next object and repeat the process. Are there books here that you will study - someday? Are there old photographs of people whom you don't know or barely remember? Are there gadgets that no longer work or which have long since lost their usefulness? Are there clothes that don't fit? Clean out your attic all the way to the walls. Rid it of all clutter. Clean the dust and debris from the corners. When it is totally clean pledge to yourself to use this quiet, clean place as a sanctuary from the senses. Leave nothing in the room that is not vibrantly alive and useful in the development of your potential. Make this room plain and simple in form, but vital and flowing in function. Keep this room empty of things, but full of no-thing. It is in this room, that you will find the infinite Tao.

Related Reading:
Section 11:1   Read 4:1, 5:2

SENSES VERSUS SELF

12:1   The five colors blind the eye.
         Racing and hunting madden the mind.
         Rare goods lead one astray.
         The five tones deafen the ear.
         The five flavors dull the tongue.

12:2   Therefore the sage's rule provides for the inner self and not for the eye.
         He rejects the one and accepts the other.

Paraphrase
12:1   A continuous overload of sensory stimulation will ultimately dull our senses. Exciting diversions cause us to constantly seek bigger thrills. The more valuable things we have, the more we want.

12:2   The sage, on the other hand, looks inward to uncover the inner self. The constant titillation of the external world is rejected and the true nature of the inner self is accepted.

For Thought:
The body is the unified whole of body and mind. Too often our acquired behavior and knowledge override our instincts. We are distracted by desire for things that we have been told are precious, only to find that when we acquire them, they are somehow not enough. So we acquire more and more while a sense of wrongness and emptiness grows with each acquisition. We literally kill ourselves pursuing the ultimate thrill of speed and danger. We try to chemically enhance senses which have been dulled by satiation. But if we allow ourselves to be driven by the external world, then we will try to ignore what is internal. The fact is, we cannot ignore our inner nature. Efforts to do so will put us into therapy and on medicine for hypertension.

For Action:
One of the great lessons of Taoism is this. The fulfillment of your potential comes from living according to inner nature and not by external stimulation. Make a list of things which you want, are pursuing, or already have. Write down five to ten items. Include material things, such as a bigger house, a luxury car, fine clothing, et cetera, which have importance to you. Also consider things such as a promotion, a bigger office, and more money. Now go through the list, item by item, and ask yourself why each one is important. Is it because you yourself think it is important and fulfilling, or is it because someone else has told you via television, advertising, or word-of-mouth that it is important. Are there any items that are directed strictly at external appearances, like a big car or an important position? Now try to assign a ranking to the items on a one to five scale, low numbers for externally directed and superficial, high numbers for internally directed and self-actualizing. Are you surprised by the result?

Related Reading:
Section 12:1   Read 3:1, 20:3
Section 12:2   Read 3:2, 19:1, 38:3, 64:5

SELFLESSNESS AND LEADERSHIP

13:1   Accept favor or disgrace with apprehension.
         Respect trouble as you do your own self.
         What is meant by accept favor or disgrace with apprehension?
         Favor is inferior.
         Be apprehensive with either its loss or gain.
         This is called accepting favor or disgrace with apprehension.
         What is meant by respect trouble as you do your own body?
         Great trouble comes from having a sense of self.
         Without a sense of self, how could there be trouble?

13:2   Therefore one who values caring for himself more than acting on behalf of the world,
         Can be trusted to care for all things.
         One who loves himself as much as the world,
         Can be trusted with the world.

Paraphrase:
13:1 Be equally apprehensive about favor and disgrace. Respect misfortunes as you do yourself. By being apprehensive about both favor and disgrace you decrease your sensitivity to both. Your sense of misfortune is centered on your body and its corresponding sense of self. Without self-centeredness you would lose your sense of personal misfortune.

13:2 People who have moved beyond both the external distractions and opinions of the world care more for their own inner life than they do for the world. These people can be trusted with the world because they attach no value to power or possessions and therefore can lead with disinterested interest.

For Thought:
Have you ever wanted something so badly that you were miserable until you got it? Once you got it were you miserable for fear you would lose it? That is what this chapter is about.

For Action:
Think back to a time when you suffered some misfortune. Consider the misfortune from an expanded, global view. Remove your self-consciousness and ego from your evaluation of the events. Look at the occurence as if it happened to someone else. Write down a description of the occurence as if you are a reporter writing a story for the paper. How great a misfortune does it seem when you consider it to be part of a natural process and do not take it personally?

Related Reading:
Section 13:1   Read 44 (all)
Section 13:2   Read 7 (all), 56:3, 78:2

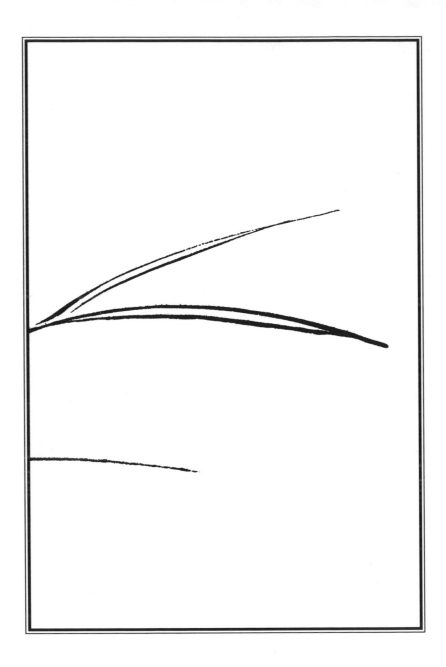

THE INVISIBLE THREAD OF TAO

14:1   Beyond seeing; its name is invisible.
        Beyond hearing; its name is inaudible.
        Beyond touching; its name is intangible.
        These three are beyond resolution,
        So they join and become one.

14:2   Viewed from above, it does not reflect.
        Viewed from below, it does not obscure.
        It goes on endlessly without name and returns to the realm beyond things.
        This is called the formless form,
        The invisible image.
        This is called elusive.
        Follow it, it has no back.
        Meet it, it has no front.

14:3   Hold on to the Tao of the present to manage the affairs of now,
        And to know the ancient beginnings.
        This is called the thread of the Tao.

Paraphrase:
14:1 The Tao has no properties which are discernible to the senses. It is a oneness that has the property of no properties.

14:2 It resembles a very thin cloud. From above, it does not reflect light. From below, it does not obscure light. Its form is so vague that you cannot see where it begins or ends.

14:3 Look behind the things of the present for the workings of Tao process. It is an unbroken thread which, when you find it, will lead back to ancient beginnings.

For Thought:
The past and future have been characterized as memories and dreams. Memories are like old photographs which, though unchanging and unchangeable, fade. Dreams are infinitely mutable, but do not always actualize. Now is the only actuality in which we can participate and, both logically and intuitively, understand.

For Action:
Look at the events going on around you. Look at personal affairs, happenings in the workplace, and the grand scale of world events. Instead of thinking of events as isolated "things" think of them as connected manifestations of an ongoing process. Pick a specific area of interest, personal, business, or world, and write down a description of the process which is unfolding behind the events. Can you tell where the process is going? How can you both expedite process and benefit from it?

Related Reading:
Section 14:1   Read 41:2, 41:3
Section 14:3   Read 21:2
Read this chapter in conjunction with Chapter 21. Read Chapter 25 for an overview of Tao process.

MYSTICAL MASTERS

15:1 The ancient masters were mystics with profound intuitive insight.
They were beyond understanding.
Because their subtlety could not be understood,
We can only describe their manifestations.
Cautious, as if crossing a wintery stream.
Hesitant, as if aware of danger.
Reserved, like a guest.
Yielding, like ice melting.
Simple, like an uncarved block.
Opaque, like muddy water.
Open, like a valley.

15:2 Muddy water, when stilled, gradually clears.
Something at rest, when moved, gradually comes alive.
Those who preserve the Tao desire not to be full.
Since they are not full they can be depleted and yet renewed.

Paraphrase:
15:1 The old masters were beyond understanding by common standards. Because of this they could only be described by external appearances. They were cautious and hesitant in their movements, never proceeding brashly. They were reserved, never calling attention to themselves. They always yielded to other's thoughts and opinions. They were simple and uncomplicated, yet opaque to understanding. They were open and receptive to all that transpired around them.

15:2 These masters knew that they could clarify their inner selves by sitting still and looking inward. They achieved ultimate stillness, and when they moved again, they were totally alive. They desired none of the fullness of the external world. Because of this, their material resources could be exhausted but they were renewed by the Tao process.

For Thought:
This chapter gives the levels in the sages' journey backward down the path. They are cautious, hesitant, reserved, yielding, simple, opaque, and open. Having progressed through the first five levels, sages become opaque to conventional wisdom because of the dissolution of the "big I" or loss of ego. To those who have been long trained to strut, act with brashness, and generally call attention to themselves, a loss of ego would be seen as lack of definition of character. But, for the Taoists who travel backward down the path, external opacity would be seen from internal stillness as remarkable clarity.

For Action:
Visualize yourself as a Taoist sage in today's world. How would you start your day? Would you read a section of the Tao Te Ching and briefly meditate on it? How would you react to the morning news? From a Taoist point of view what is important in current events and what is not? Are there ways of dealing with people which are not dominating, unyielding, or motion oriented? Can you sit still to achieve clarity in a muddy situation and then act with tremendous life and potency? Visualize all this, then conduct part, if not all, of your day using your Taoist vision.

Related Reading:
Section 15:1   Read 69:1
Section 15:2   Read 9:1, 22:1, 29:1, 30:2, 45:1, 55:3

STILLNESS AND CONSTANCY

16:1   Attain the utmost emptiness.
        Maintain the deepest stillness.
        All things rise to activity,
        And I watch their return.
        They come forth and flourish,
        Then return to their origin.
        Returning to one's origin is stillness.
        Stillness is the fullfillment of one's nature.
        Fullfilling one's nature is to be constant.

16:2   Constancy yields insight.
        Lack of constancy yields disaster.
        Insight leads to enlightenment,
        Enlightenment leads to impartiality,
        Impartiality leads to power,
        Power leads to oneness with nature,
        Oneness with nature leads to the Tao.
        When eternally with the Tao,
        One will not come to harm throughout life.

Paraphrase:
16:1 Empty yourself of your self. Maintain stillness. All things rise to activity from the
empty stillness of their origins. They grow and flourish and then return to their source.
You can return to your source by practicing stillness. Through this stillness you can fulfill your natural potential. To do so is to have constancy of purpose.

16:2 Constancy of purpose yields insight. Not knowing constancy of purpose leads to
disaster. Constancy of purpose leads to tolerance of all things. Tolerance leads to disinterested interest. Dispassionate unity with things leads to the power to rule. The power
to rule leads to sacred power. Sacred power carries one to the Tao process. Being at one
with the Tao process taps the eternal. Tapping the eternal removes harm from the
events of one's life.

For Thought:
All activities in nature are cyclical. All things rise to activity and then return to the empty
stillness of their origins. One can return to one's transcendental origins by stillness and
thereby find fulfillment. There are no easy answers to great mysteries. The fulfillment of
one's nature requires constancy of purpose.

For Action:
Find a quiet place and time and practice stillness. Relax and be quiet. Then be quieter.
Empty yourself of your self. Don't concentrate. Concentration requires consciousness of
self. Just be empty. Just be. Walk into the spiral labyrinth of your being. The walls block
out the distractions of your senses but the top is open to the cosmic sky. Look up as you
move in to the center of stillness, the heart of emptiness. Do this meditation repeatedly.

Related Reading:
Section 16:1   Read 21:1, 25 (all), 40 (all), 65:2
Section 16:2   Read 33:2, 52:1, 52:3, 55:2, 59 (all)

QUALITIES OF LEADERSHIP

17:1   The best leader is barely known to man.
        Next comes the leader who is known and praised,
        Then the one who is feared,
        Then the one who is despised.

17:2   He who mistrusts will not be trusted.

17:3   The wise leader speaks little and does so cautiously.
        When his task is accomplished,
        People say that they did it themselves.

Paraphrase:
17:1 The best leaders stay in the background while quietly facilitating process. Next come the ones who take pride in their great working relationship with their subordinates. Then come the autocratic, arbitrary leaders who strike fear in their followers. Finally there are incompetent leaders who are despised for their ineptitude.

17:2 Those who habitually mistrust themselves and others will not inspire trust.
17:3 Wise leaders do not talk a lot. They carefully consider the words that they will use before they speak. Because they facilitate and do not dictate, when the work is done people say that they did it by themselves.

For Thought:
This applies to modern management theory. Leaders who are known and praised are Theory Y managers. Those who are feared are Theory X managers. Unfortunately there are many managers who are incompetent and therefore despised. The best leaders are in none of these categories. These leaders direct their efforts toward understanding process and thus move beyond praise, fear, or derision. They are open-minded and trust others to help them to understand the process they manage. They are careful in what they say because they know that if they are loved by some, they will be hated by others. They coach, facilitate, and lead by example.

For Action:
Get a book on management and read about Theory X and Theory Y. Make a step by step, beginning to end flow chart of the process which you lead or manage.

Related Reading:
Section 17:1   Read 58:1, 72 (all)
Section 17:2   Read 23:1, 27:2, 56 (all)

DEGENERATION

18:1   When the great Tao is left behind,
        Kindness and morality appear.
        When knowledge and cleverness come forth,
        Great hypocrisy follows.
        When families fall into disharmony,
        Piety and devotion ensue.
        When a country is in chaos and disorder,
        Loyal ministers are praised.

Paraphrase:
18:1 When we move away from spontaneous participation in the Tao process all sorts of superficiality and sophistry take over. Self-serving, self-righteous morality replaces natural goodness. Abstraction replaces hands-on doing. Piety replaces loving concern. Politicians replace leaders.

For Thought:
This chapter is about superficiality versus substance. When we turn away from the Tao process we begin to react to mental constructs of reality instead of reality. Instead of following the deepest intuition or sense of rightness in ourselves, we intellectualize morality and benevolence. We reward clever come-backs more than wise words. We are more concerned with names than nature.

For Action:
I have a smooth black stone which my daughter gave to me. It is marbled with a tracery of white. The slip of paper which came with it says that it is snowflake obsidian and that it represents harmony in the contrast of dark and light, yin and yang. I kept the slip of paper so that I would know what the stone is. Now I realize that this is a symptom of the conditioning which I have undergone since childhood. I have to name everything so that I know what it is. But naming my snowflake obsidian tells me nothing about its nature. To know its nature I must put away the slip and pick up the stone. How does it feel? Is it sharp-cornered? Does it have an odor? Is it heavy in my hand? Does it reflect light? Even if I wrote down answers to all these questions I would still not capture the nature of this stone. I cannot describe the stoneness of snowflake obsidian to you. I can only hand you the stone. Now find something for which you have a name. Forget the name and interact with it. Remove your ego, disconnect your logic circuits, and interact with this thing. Get to know its nature.

Related Reading:
Section 18:1   Read 19:1, 38:2, 38:3

PLAIN AND SIMPLE

19:1   Discard knowledge and its cunning,
        People will benefit a hundredfold.
        Discard morality and its righteousness,
        People will return to family duty and love.
        Discard cleverness and its profit,
        There will be no more thieves and robbers.
        These three things are superficial and deficient.
        It is more important to:
        Show plainess and hold to simplicity,
        Reduce selfishness and limit desires,
        Give up learning and sorrows end.

Paraphrase:
19:1 Give up erudition and sophistry and people will benefit greatly. Discard artificial morality and righteousness and people will return to duty and love. Discard clever strategy and its profit and people will not steal. These three things are inadequate. It is more important to display plainess and the simple self, to reduce self-centeredness and limit desires. Give up learned behavior and sorrows end.

For Thought:
These days it seems that there is a technique for everything. Books on management technique abound. There are even books with strategies for out-flanking those who are using strategies from earlier books. Intensive three-day workshops and five-day courses promise to teach us how to conduct our lives, become rich and famous, and rule the world. Forget techniques! They are hollow.

For Action:
Conduct your business and personal relationships today on instinct and intuition. Ask yourself if the messages you send are pure or if they are contaminated with emotional baggage and attitudes. Be aware of the voice inside you which tells you about the rightness or wrongness of situations and interactions. Do not suppress that voice with intellectualization, rationalization, or ego. Perceive and acknowledge true, unadorned potentiality within yourself. Search for the central, true self in others. Draw it out if possible, and nurture it. Give up the mistrust and selfishness taught by society. Remember to trust yourself and it will be easier to trust others.

Related Reading:
Section 19:1   Read 3:3, 48:1, 57:2, 57:3, 65:2, 71:1

BEING DIFFERENT

20:1   How much difference is there between yes and no?
How much difference is there between beauty and ugliness?

20:2   He who is feared must also fear.
Wild desolation! It will never end!

20:3   Other people are joyful,
As if enjoying a banquet,
As if climbing up to a terrace in spring.
I alone am inactive and uninvolved,
Like an infant still unable to smile,
Unattached like one with no place to go.
Other people are affluent.
I alone have nothing.
I am foolish and confused.
Ordinary people are bright.
I am dull.
Ordinary people are clever and self-assured.
I am dismal and subdued.
I am formless like the ocean,
I am shapeless and unbounded.
Other people pursue a goal.
I alone am mulish and awkward.
My desires alone differ from other people's.
I am sustained by the mother.

Paraphrase:
20:1   The dualities of yes and no, beauty and ugliness are but two sides of the same coin.
How much difference is there, really?

20:2   Those who are feared because of their power, position, and possessions must ultimately fear those who have more. It is an endless spiral of emptiness.

20:3   People are joyful in consumption and pursuit of power. I do not share such actions. I am like a baby who is uninterested. I am a stranger in a strange land. People are affluent. I have nothing and appear foolish because of this. People have happy faces and bright clothes. I am dull by comparison. They are clever and self-confident. I am dismal and retiring. I do not have the well-formed values that they have and, thus, seem shapeless. They pursue a common goal which I stubbornly resist. To them I am uncouth and unsophisticated. What I desire is different. I am sustained by the mother principle of Tao.

For Thought:
We are conditioned by mass media and mass advertising to fear being different. While it is true that the rich and powerful tend to fear those who are more rich and powerful, it is also true that they fear those who simply choose not to play the game. This is fearsome to vested interests because it exposes the superficiality of the trappings of society.

For Action:
Some time during the day take a few moments and imagine yourself to be like Data on Star Trek: The Next Generation. Evaluate what is going on around you in a totally detached, logical way. Determine for yourself what is important. Will you be a better person dressed in one type of clothing or another? Will your inner self be enhanced by your possessions? Must you be part of an in-group to survive? Are you showing your true self to your friends and family? Use logic to look behind superficiality. Use intuition to see the path with a heart.

Related Reading:
Section 20:3   Read 52:1

THE PREGNANT TAO

21.

21:1   The inherent quality of virtue comes from the Tao alone.

21:2   The Tao is elusive and vague.
        Vague and elusive,
        Yet within, are images;
        Elusive and vague,
        Yet within, are things;
        Shadowy and dark,
        Yet within, are essences.
        The essences are real and hold the truth.
        From now back to antiquity its name persists,
        And is a means of viewing the origin of all things.

        How do I know the origin of all things?
        Because of this.

Paraphrase:
21:1   The inherent characteristics and potential of all things come from the Tao
alone.

21:2   The Tao is not easy to see and understand. Think of it as an infinite creative
principle. It contains the plan and organization of all things. The essences and processes of the present are real and can be used to trace a path backward to their ancient origins. Because of this we can have an intuitive understanding of the origin of all things.

For Thought:
Virtue as creative power and potential, such as is found in a seed, comes from and is a
manifestation of Tao. In this chapter we glimpse the creative process of Tao.

For Action:
Are there meanings for the word virtue that have no connection with morality? Look up
the word and see. While you have the dictionary out look up the word logos. It might
help you to understand the Tao process. Finally, for a parallel in Western thought, read
John 1:1-5.

Related Reading:
Section 21:1   Read 40:2
Section 21:2   Read 54:3
Read this chapter together with Chapter 14. Read Chapter 25 for an overview of Tao
process.

YIELD AND BECOME WHOLE

22:1   Yield and become whole,
         Bend and become straight,
         Be empty and become filled,
         Be exhausted and become renewed.
         Have little and receive much,
         Have much and be confused.

22:2   Therefore the sage holds to the one,
         And is an example to all.
         He does not show off and thus is conspicuous.
         He is not self-righteous and thus is distinguished.
         He does not brag and thus is credited.
         He is not proud and thus endures.
         He does not contend and no one contends with him.
         When the ancients said to yield and become whole,
         Their words were close to the mark.
         He is always whole.

Paraphrase:
22:1   Yield and overcome. Be flexible and you will straighten, after the external
stress is removed. Empty yourself of your self and you will be filled by the Tao process.
Exhaust your wilfulness and your spirit will be renewed. Have few material goods and
you will receive great benefits. Have many material goods and you will be distracted
constantly.

22:2   Sages hold to unity with the Tao process and thus lead all. They call no attention to themselves and are conspicuous for doing so. They are humble and thus draw
honor to themselves. They do not argue and thus no one wants to argue with them. By
yielding they overcome and thus they are always whole.

For Thought:
I have been told that the name of one of the martial arts translates as the way of the
green stick. This nicely brings home the premise that, if you bend, you will not break.

For Action:
Sometimes we say that we will not compromise our principles when, what we mean is
that we are stiffened with pride. Sometimes we argue our case when we are really hard-
ened with ego. To overcome both internal and external obstacles, consciously practice
yielding. Yield to the demands of other people's egoes to overcome your own. Allow
other people to be proud to empty yourself of pride. Do not argue with the argumentive
and they will not have cause to argue with you. Practice yielding daily and you will overcome.

Related Reading:
Section 22:1   Read 15:2, 45:1, 78:1
Section 22:2   Read 8:3, 24 (all), 66:4

BRIEF SPEECH, HIGH EXPECTATIONS *23.*

23:1   Brevity in speech emulates nature.
        A high wind does not last all morning,
        A rainstorm does not last all day.
        What causes this?
        If nature cannot make things last long,
        How much less can man?

23:2   Therefore those who follow the Tao,
        Identify with the Tao.
        Those who follow virtue,
        Identify with virtue.
        Those who follow loss,
        Identify with loss.
        To those who identify with virtue,
        The Tao gives virtue.
        To those who identify with loss,
        The Tao gives loss.

Paraphrase:
23:1   It is unnatural to talk too much. If natural phenomena don't go on and on, why should we?

23:2   You derive from the Tao process exactly what you put into it. If you develop your potential, you will discover your vast potentiality. If you expect failure, you will fail.

For Thought:
We live in a world full of words. We are bombarded with messages from all quarters. Unfortunately many of the messages which we receive are scant in meaning, superficial, self-serving, and largely false. How much quieter the world would be if everyone spoke only when they had something to say which would educate, illuminate, and help everyone who heard.

For Action:
Practice listening. In the next conversation which you have with someone, try to judge whether you or the other person speaks more. Think about what you say. Could it be said with equal clarity in fewer words?

Related Reading:
Section 23:1   Read 5:3, 17:3, 24:1, 45:3, 56 (all)

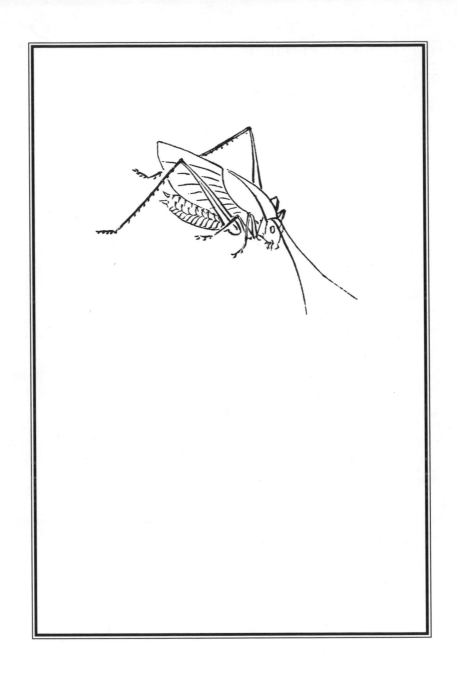

THE FAILURE OF EGO

24:1   One who boasts is not steady.
        One who shows off is not distinguished.
        One who puts on a display cannot illuminate.
        One who boasts will not succeed.
        One who brags will not make enduring achievements.
        To those who follow the Tao,
        These actions are like surplus and redundancy.
        They are despised.
        Therefore one who possesses the Tao leaves them behind.

Paraphrase:
24:1   Those who boast display inner uncertainty. Those who show off lose presence
and leadership ability. Boasting and bragging assure failure and alienation. All of these
things are symptoms of the failure of ego. To sages these things are extra baggage and
do not bring happiness. Thus sages turn away from ego.

For Thought:
Just as action produces reaction, calling attention to oneself will cause people to turn
away. So boasting, bragging, and showing off cause others to look for and find one's
shortcomings.

For Action:
Keep a mental score as you go through today. How many people brag, boast, and show
off? Try to see inside them and understand why they are bragging. Look inside yourself
and evaluate what you intend to say next. Is it loaded with the "big I"?

Related Reading:
Section 24:1   Read 2:2, 9:1, 22:2, 30:1, 72:3

THE TAO PROCESS

25.

25:1   Something formless yet complete,
Existed before the universe,
Silent and still,
Alone and unchanging.
It may be regarded as the mother of all things.
I do not know how to name it.
I will identify it as the Tao.
If I am forced to name it,
I will call it great.
Great also means moving on,
Moving on requires going far,
Going far requires returning.

25:2   Tao is great,
Heaven is great,
Earth is great,
And the leader is great.
These are four parts to greatness,
And one belongs to the leader.

25:3   Man imitates earth,
Earth imitates heaven,
Heaven imitates Tao,
Tao imitates itself.

Paraphrase:
25:1   Before the universe there was a formless void which was complete in itself. Because it produced the universe it may be regarded as the mother of all things. We will call it Tao and witness its process. Things come from it, go on their way, and then return to be absorbed in it.

25:2   Tao is great. The metaphysical and physical, which are two manifestations of the Tao, are great. The leader who mediates the physical and metaphysical is also great.

25:3   The organization and evolution of human culture take on the natural form of the rest of physical nature. Physical nature mirrors natural law. Natural law arises from the Tao process. The Tao process is self-sufficient.

For Thought:
The sequence in 25:3 shows that we are a microcosm of the grand progression from mankind to nature to natural law to Tao process. Thus, if one could walk backward down the path, peeling away layers of consciousness, one might come to the center of one's soul to find nothing and everything.

For Action:
Think about what you've read about Tao and Tao process. Write your own summary. Don't worry if it seems vague or incomplete. As your understanding grows, both logical and intuitive, you will come back to this chapter.

Related Reading:
Section 25:1   Read 16:1
Section 25:3   Read 34 (all)

CALM STILLNESS, SOUND BASIS

26.

26:1   The heavy is the foundation of the light,
         The still is the master of movement.
         Therefore a gentleman travels all day,
         Without losing sight of his baggage.
         When surrounded by the distractions of a hostel,
         He remains calm and detached.
         How then can the lord of ten thousand chariots act foolishly in public?
         To act foolishly is to lose one's foundation.
         To be agitated is to lose one's self-mastery.

Paraphrase:
26:1   Everything of substance has a heavy foundation. All activity has its root in still
planning. Thus sages may go forth but they never will lose sight of their foundation.
Even when surrounded by pleasant sights and warm company they remain calm and
detached. How then can our leaders act foolishly before the public eye? To do so is to
lose one's basis. To be agitated is to show lack of self-mastery.

For Thought:
Calm stillness allows one to focus on Tao process. Focus leads to understanding.
Understanding leads to enlightenment. Enlightenment allows one to become a leader
because he or she has a sound basis.

For Action:
Today, when you face a difficult problem or situation, remember this chapter. As you
work through the difficulty remember that a moment of stillness will assure correct
action. So, before you launch into activity, stop. Calm yourself and, if you are emotional-
ly involved in the situation, step back into detachment. Focus on the process which is
the foundation of the activities and events before you. Don't be agitated if the solution
or correct action doesn't come to you immediately. Create a small bubble of calm stillness around you, and a sound basis for your actions will surface in your mind.

Related Reading:
Section 26:1   Read 45:2, 45:3

RESPECTING COMPETENCE, TREASURING RESOURCES

27:1   A good walker leaves no tracks.
A good speaker speaks flawlessly.
A good reckoner needs no counters.
A well-shut door cannot be opened though there are no bolts or bars.
A well-tied knot cannot be untied though there are no cords or twine.

27:2   Therefore the sage attends to everyone and rejects no one.
He attends to all things and wastes nothing.
This is called double enlightenment.

27:3   The good man is the teacher of the good man.
The bad man is the resource of the good man.
If one does not respect his teacher,
If one does not treasure his resource,
Then, though he is educated, he is foolish.
This is the essential mystery.

Paraphrase:
27:1   The greatest competence leaves no trace of its activity. It uses all its resources to produce a perfect and economical result.

27:2   Sages, in the same manner, attend to everyone and everything. Nothing is wasted. This the double light of both competence and stewardship.

27:3 The good person is both teacher and student. The bad person is a resource and an opportunity for the good person. One should respect competence in one's teacher and treasure the opportunity provided by one's student. Failure to do so negates erudition and makes one the wise fool. This is paradoxical but true.

For Thought:
Have you ever been awe stricken at the effortlessness of true competence? I have seen speakers who were so good that they called no attention to themselves and thus enhanced understanding of their message. This type of performance requires total use of all resources to produce remarkable effects.

For Action:
Pick one task or aspect of your job which you will perform today. Try to step outside yourself and watch yourself working. Is there waste of resources or time? Do you find yourself backtracking or repeating parts of the work? Do you write things down and then lose your notes? Are you using equipment and training for maximum efficiency and effectiveness? After analyzing your performance try to think through your task and to visualize new and improved ways to do it. Go after inefficiency and waste with a vengeance. Practice economy of motion. See how your work and your perception of yourself improve.

Related Reading:
Section 27:1   Read 8:2, 17:1
Section 27:2   Read 49:2, 62:1, 62:2, 62:3
Section 27:3   Read 52:3

BALANCED SIMPLICITY, CONSTANT POTENTIAL

28:1   Know the male, but keep to the female,
And become the watercourse to the world.
Be the watercourse to the world,
And constant virtue will not desert you.
You will return to the state of a new born child.
Know the pure but keep to the sullied,
And become the valley to the world.
Be the valley to the world,
And your constant virtue will be complete.
When your constant virtue is complete,
You will return to the state of the uncarved block.
Know the white but keep to the dark,
And become a benchmark to the world.
Be a benchmark to the world,
And your constant virtue will not waver.
When your constant virtue is unwavering,
You will return to the state of the uncreated void.

28:2   When the uncarved block is split it becomes tools.
When the sage is used, he becomes lord over the officials.
But great carving cuts little.

Paraphrase:
28:1   Maintain balance between your masculine and feminine principles and all things will come to you. You will have infinite potential like that of an infant. Remember that good and bad are relative to each other. Maintain balance in your evaluation of things and all things will come to you. Your potential will be complete. You will return to the simple, natural state of human nature. Know both active and passive in yourself and others and you will become an example to the world. By being an example you will fulfill your potential. You will achieve unity with the Tao process.
28:2   When simple unity is broken into components it becomes tools for use. When sages are used they become leaders of leaders. But as leaders, sages do little to alter natural process.

For Thought:
When the sage is used in an organization he or she becomes a leader. The most effective leader is the one least changed by leadership. The sage is effective because of his or her ability to be a channel or watercourse. Disconnected information and effort flows through the leader to become collected, coherent, and potent. Just as a great carver cuts little, the sage doesn't modify effort and information. He or she only collects and correlates. Then the answers come, and process flows.

For Action:
In your work or interactions are you ever overwhelmed with the number of problems, amount of information, and the disconnected effort going on around you? Often I respond to this chaos by thinking of new controls or reports that will solve the problem or direct the effort. But it may be wiser to find ways to more efficiently collect and correlate existing information. What does the information which you are getting really pertain to? Instead of more information, maybe you need less extraneous information. What exactly is the problem and what are its possible causes? What effort could be redirected to solve the problem? Remember to see simplicity in the complicated and to establish order before disorder sets in.

Related Reading:
Section 28:1   Read 6 (all), 10:1, 32:2, 41:2, 66:1
Section 28:2   Read 32:1

TAMPERING WITH THE WORLD

29:1   If one tries to act upon the world,
            He will not succeed.
            The world is a sacred vessel and should not be tampered with.
            He who acts upon the world destroys it.
            He who grasps the world loses it.

29:2   In the world:
            Some things lead, some follow;
            Some blow hot, some blow cold;
            Some are strong, some are weak;
            Some are steady, and some are unstable.

29:3   Therefore the sage avoids extremes, excesses, and extravagances.

Paraphrase:
29:1   The more we try to alter nature to our own specifications, the less successful we will be. The world is a sacred, living organism. When we tamper with it, we kill part of it. If we continue to tamper, we will kill it all and, with it, ourselves.

29:2   Everything is part of a natural balance. There are leaders and followers, strong and weak, static and dynamic.

29:3   The wise person avoids all extreme positions, excessive consumption, and extravagant expenditures.

For Thought:
The world is a living organism of which we are a part. Many of the earliest religions centered around the earth as a sacred vessel which operated in a continuous cycle of birth, life, death, and rebirth. In these religions, vestiges of which still survive today, there was an I-thou relationship between mankind and nature. People, living things, and even inanimate objects were approached with a sacred awe which rendered the most mundane acts into mystical, religious experience. We must return to this simple vision. We must recognize that we are not apart from nature with dominion over it. We are part of nature with the responsibility for its stewardship.

For Action:
Is sacred the same as divine? Look up both words. What is the difference between domination and stewardship? Look up both words. For a thought from the Judeo-Christian tradition which is similar to the one expressed in 29:2, read Ecclesiastes 3:1-8.

Related Reading:
Section 29:1   Read 47 (all), 48 (all), 57 (all), 64:3
Section 29:3   Read 24 (all), 30 (all), 55:3

ACHIEVING WITHOUT CONQUERING

30:1   He who uses the Tao to advise a ruler will oppose violence.
        Such methods tend to turn on the user.
        Briars grow where armies have been.
        The good general only achieves what has to be done.
        He does not use force for his own gain.
        He achieves results without boasting;
        He achieves results without pride;
        He achieves results without bragging;
        He achieves results as a matter of necessity;
        This is called achieving results without conquering.

30:2   Developing excessive strength hastens decay.
        This is contrary to the Tao.
        Things contrary to the Tao soon cease to be.

Paraphrase:
30:1   The Tao process abhors violence. Violence enacted brings violence in return.
So, if pushed to a fight, do only what is necessary. Do not pursue an advantage for self-
serving reasons. Achieve results without boasting, bragging, or undue pride. Do what
you have to do of necessity but without excessive force and with no expectation of
abject submission.

30:2 Pursuit of excessive strength for purposes of conquering assures rapid decay.
Conquering is a disruption of Tao process. Things which disrupt the Tao process soon
perish.

For Thought:
Our culture in the West is permeated with hostility and aggression. Our tendencies are
to conquer everything from our neighbors to nature itself. Remember that living by violence means dying by violence. Ultimately the conqueror will lose strength and old ene-
mies will return to conquer. How much better would it be if results could be achieved
with accomodation instead of acrimony.

For Action:
Have you become desensitized to violence and aggression? Probably you have. Think
about the events that occur around you and in which you participate today. Ask yourself
how much aggression and violence, physical or symbolic, is contained in each event.
While driving to work did you pass someone or have someone pass you? If so, was it
because of time or was it a symbolic expression of aggressive superiority? Did you
demand that a subordinate perform some menial task that you could have done yourself? Was it necessity or hostility that guided your actions? Are you and the people
around you super-fans of sports? Why is it important that this team or that team wins a
game? Does participation in vicarious aggression really make you feel better about yourself? How many people did you see get killed today in T.V. dramas? How many guns
were fired? How many rapes and muggings were perpetrated? Is all this violence enrich-
ing your life?

Related Reading:
Section 30:1   Read 31:1, 42:5, 76:2
Section 30:2   Read 9 (all), 29:3, 55:3

SADNESS IN VICTORY

31:1   Weapons are tools of evil which are hated by many.
        Therefore followers of the Tao reject them.
        The wise man prefers the left in times of peace.
        He prefers the right in times of war.
        Weapons are instruments of destruction.
        They are not normally used by a wise man.
        When he uses them of necessity, he does so with calm detachment,
        And does not see them as things of beauty.
        To see weapons as things of beauty is to delight in killing.
        Whoever delights in killing cannot inherit the earth.
        Thus the left is preferred on happy occasions.
        The right is preferred on sad occasions.
        So the second in command stands on the left,
        While the commander stands on the right.
        This means that victory in war is observed like a funeral.
        The victims of war should be mourned in grief and sorrow.
        That is why victory is treated like a funeral.

Paraphrase:
31:1   Weapons are tools of evil and are rejected by followers of the Tao. Sages prefer
the pacifist feminine principle to the war-like masculine principle. When forced into
conflict, sages use weapons with calm detachment. They see no beauty in weapons nor
delight in killing. Those who delight in killing are not fit to lead. Wise leaders see sadness in victory.

For Thought:
In the morning paper I read a brief story entitled "Effort to Fire Census Worker Dropped".
The Census Bureau, in the face of public scrutiny, dropped efforts to fire a demographer
who released estimates of Iraqui deaths in the Persian Gulf war. She estimated that
86,194 men, 39,612 women, and 32,195 children died as a result of the war and its after-
math. These numbers tend to take the edge off of our national celebration of victory and
our pride in weapons technologies such as Stealth bombers and smart bombs. Perhaps
mourning and sadness are more in order for our victory.

For Action:
Conflict in personal and business relationships is in effect a small war. Using wits or
strategy to overcome your opponent may win a small victory but the war will continue.
When you sense conflict with someone, think of ways to defuse it. Use facilitation
instead of acrimony. Remember, if you win in a conflict, someone lost. If the winner rev-
els, the loser will retaliate.

Related Reading:
Section 31:1   Read 30 (all), 69:3

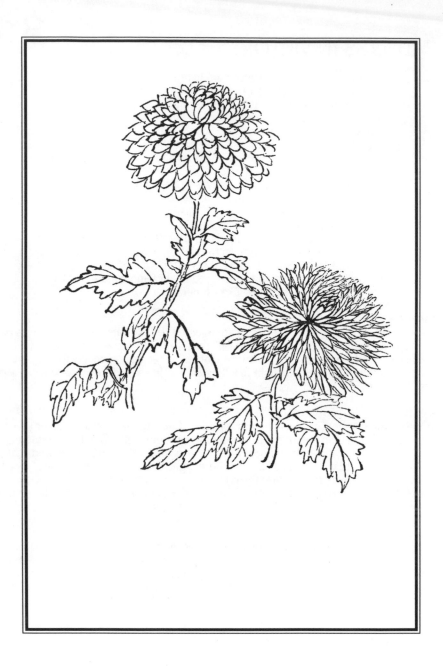

SIMPLICITY AND ITS LOSS

32.

32:1   The Tao is forever unnamed.
        In its original simplicity it cannot be exploited.
        If leaders could keep its simplicity,
        Then all people would honor and obey them.
        Heaven and earth would combine to produce a sweet dew,
        Which would fall, beyond anyone's command, equally on all men.
        When the original simplicity is lost, names arise.
        Once there are names one must know when to stop.
        Knowing when to stop frees one from danger.

32:2   Tao is to the world like valley streams are to rivers and the sea.

Paraphrase:
32:1   The Tao process is. It is the natural flow of things, and in its vastness it is the
ultimate simplicity. If leaders could acknowledge the original simplicity, then people
would willingly follow them. The rewards of natural process would come to everyone
without artificial distinctions. But when the original simplicity is lost artificial distinctions are made and everything is tagged with a name. The more names there are, the
more complicated and convoluted things become. So one must know when to say
enough is enough. Thus the complexities and problems associated with too many
names can be avoided.

32:2   The Tao process carries and accumulates all things in a natural flow.

For Thought:
Man is an inveterate tinkerer. I was once talking to a paint formulator who told me that
he could tell how old a product was by the number of ingredients in its formulation. He
went on to explain that no one ever took anything out of a formulation when a problem
arose. Instead some ingredient would be added. Sometimes two of the added ingredients would interact to create a new problem and yet another ingredient would be added.
There is always one more law to be written, one more machine to be invented, and one
more chemical to be produced. When is enough, enough?

For Action:
Think about something which you do at home or work. Write down the steps required to
accomplish the objective. Are any of the steps redundant? Could they be done in another order to achieve the same goal with less time and energy expended? Simplify the
process as much as possible. Then try doing it exactly as you planned it. Keep at it until
the ultimate simplicity is achieved. Remember, there is one best way to do anything. By
systematically simplifying you can find it.

Related Reading:
Section 32:1   Read 9 (all), 15:1, 28 (all), 35:1, 37:1, 44 (all)
Section 32:2   Read 34:1, 66:1

OVERCOMING SELF

33:1   One who understands others is knowledgeable.
        One who understands oneself is enlightened.
        One who overcomes others has power.
        One who overcomes oneself has inner strength.

33:2   One who is content is wealthy.
        One who perserveres has constancy of purpose.
        One who maintains one's position in life endures.
        One who dies, but is not forgotten has longevity.

Paraphrase:
33:1   It is good to understand others' behavior, but it is more enlightened to understand your own. You can demonstrate raw power by overcoming others. By overcoming
yourself you demonstrate pure inner strength.

33:2   Contentment is wealth. Perserverence shows constancy of purpose. If you hold
fast to these principles, you will endure. Your memory will live on after you die.

For Thought:
Adages and aphorisms constantly remind us to know ourselves and to be true to ourselves. Yet how much time do you spend seeking insight through in-sight?

For Action:
Think about someone with whom you have close contact either on a personal or professional basis. Write down a brief description of the character traits that you see in that
person. Does he or she display too much ego? Is he or she defensive, aggressive, passive, or dominating? What does that person need to grow? Now look at yourself in the
same way. Go through the same list of traits. What do you need to do to grow and fulfill
your potential?

Related Reading:
Section 33:2   Read 16 (all), 44:1, 46:2, 52:3, 54 (all), 59 (all)

SMALL IN DESIRE, GREAT IN ACTION

34:1   The Tao is pervasive, flowing on the left and on the right.
It works and completes its affairs but never lays claim.
All things return to it but it never acts as master.
Ever desireless it is small.
All things return to it, but it never acts as master.
It is great.
Therefore the sage can accomplish great things,
Because he does not attempt to be great,
And therefore is truly great.

Paraphrase:
34:1   The Tao is omnipresent. The Tao process proceeds naturally and spontaneously without consciousness or design. All things return to it because they are part of it, yet it never acts as master. Because it is not corporate, it is small. Everything is part of it, so it is infinite. The sage can accomplish great things by emulating the Tao process. True greatness is assured by not attempting to be great.

For Thought:
The Tao process is like a great breaking wave in the ocean. The present reality is at the break. It is full of action. It is dynamic and represents the release of great potential energy. Its kinetics are complex and ever-changing. Its power carries us forward into the void that is the future. Now occupied, the void becomes the present. Then the wave moves on and it becomes part of the great ocean of the past. Ride the wave into the future. Learn to use its power because your own power is inconsequential in the face of it. Learn to tap the vast pool of human memory and capability which is the past. From it you will draw sustenance, energy, understanding, and ultimately, real meaning.

For Action:
Think about people in your life for whom you have respect and admiration. Pick the one who stands out the most as a leader. Write down the leadership traits which this person exhibits. Does he or she rule by dictatorial edict? Is this person more likely to say or to do? Does he or she coach people by personal example? Do you think that this person is a leader through planned effort or through natural capability? Would you like to be a leader? Then forget leadership and concentrate on learning about the process going on around you.

Related Reading:
Section 34:1   Read 2:2, 7:2, 10:2, 16:1, 25:1, 25:2, 51 (all), 63:4, 77:2

HIDDEN PROCESS,
INEXHAUSTIBLE USE

35:1   Keep to the great form and all the world will come.
         It will come without harm in safety and peace.

35:2   When music and fine food are offered,
         Strangers will stop in.
         Thus, when told of the Tao,
         We say it seems tasteless and bland.
         We look, but cannot see it.
         We listen, but cannot hear it.
         We use it, but cannot exhaust it.

Paraphrase:
35:1   By studying and understanding the great Tao process everything will come to you. Because you see the underlying nature of things, they will not harm you and peace will surround you.

35:2   People who are strangers to you and the Tao, are attracted by sensual pleasures such as food and music. But mention the Tao and they are turned off by its subtlety. They don't realize that, although it is hidden from the senses, it is an inexhaustible source of usefulness.

For Thought:
This chapter brings out a key idea for the practice of Taoism. It is the notion that one can function practically and effectively in the real world while holding to the fundamental principles of the Tao process. In fact, comprehension of this process will allow you to see beneath the superficialities of the world of the senses and to avoid the traps and pitfalls to which the majority of people succumb. Being a Taoist does not require monastic asceticism. It implies only that you comprehend the Tao process and that your actions in the world mirror your level of understanding.

For Action:
A parallel to the thought in this chapter exists in the theme of the mystical Jesus. Read Matthew 13:10-17.

Related Reading:
Section 35:1   Read 32:1, 37:1
Section 35:2   Read 4:1, 6:1, 14:1, 41:3, 45:1, 63:1

WEAKNESS IN STRENGTH, STRENGTH IN WEAKNESS

36:1 In order to make a thing smaller,
You must first expand it.
In order to weaken it,
You must first strengthen it.
In order to abandon it,
You must first work closely with it.
In order to take from it,
You must first give to it.
This is called subtle enlightenment.
The soft and weak overcome the strong.

36:2 As fish should not leave deep water,
So should the sharp instruments of state not be revealed.

Paraphrase:
36:1 When a thing reaches the limit of its expansion it can only contract. There is a weakness in the greatest strength. Great familiarity with a thing makes it easy to abandon it. Giving to something assures that you will receive from it. It is subtle enlightenment to see the weakness in strength and to know the strength of weakness.

36:2 Just as fish should not leave deep water, one should carefully conceal one's strategy and strength.

For Thought:
The first part of this chapter is a continuation of the theme of growth and decay as the essence of natural Tao process. When a thing travels to the far limits of its potential then it can only return to its weakest origins. The second part of the chapter carries forward the theme that if one keeps one's strength and strategy hidden, then they are less likely to create strong reaction and counter-strategy in others. When a well-hidden strength is revealed in the face of threat or oppression, your oppressor will be surprised and off-balance as a result.

For Action:
Practice going far and then returning in your daily activities and interactions. If you freely give to someone, they will return in kind. If you are yielding to someone now, later they will willingly yield to you. It is said that familiarity breeds contempt. Thus the more acquainted you are with something, the more likely you are to see why you can be without it. You can't always be strong. Yield in the face of superior strength and you will discover the strength in your weakness.

Related Reading.
Section 36:1   Read 30:2, 43:1, 52:3, 76 (all), 78:1
Section 36:2   Read 57 (all)

RIGHTNESS AND SIMPLICITY

37.

37:1　　The Tao is forever unnamed,
　　　　Yet nothing remains undone.
　　　　If leaders could keep its simplicity,
　　　　Then all people would transform themselves.
　　　　If, after their transformation, they should rise to action,
　　　　I shall restrain them with the nameless simplicity.
　　　　The nameless simplicity subdues without disgrace.
　　　　Absence of disgrace leads to stillness,
　　　　And the world rights itself of its own accord.

Paraphrase:
37:1　　The underlying Tao process simply is. Although amazingly complicated in detail, it is profoundly simple in function. Everything is done within its context without huge effort or ingenious plan. Leaders fall to the temptation to be tamperers. They tinker, tweak, and legislate, but since they can't agree among themselves, all the grand actions fail. It would be no disgrace if everyone would tamper less and facilitate more. Then people would work out most of their own problems.

For Thought:
The function of Tao process is to make all other processes self-ordering and self-balancing. People who understand this natural tendency toward rightness will use a self-imposed restraint to control their urge to tamper. Thus they avoid the disgrace of failure. They can rejoin the stillness of the Tao process without injury to pride and without stigma.

For Action:
Think of a time when you meddled or tinkered in someone's affairs. Write down details of what you did and what the outcome was. Was the outcome what you expected? What do you think would have happened if you had not become involved? What did you gain and what did you lose by your action? What did others gain or lose?

Related Reading:
Section 37:1　　　Read 2:2, 3:3, 32:1, 35:1, 48 (all), 57:3

RIGHTNESS AND RITES

38:1 A person of high virtue is unaware of virtue,
And therefore has true virtue.
A person of low virtue never loses sight of virtue,
And therefore has no virtue.
A person of high virtue does not act,
And has no reason for acting.
A person of high benevolence acts,
And has no reason for acting.
A person of high righteousness acts,
And has a reason for acting.
A person of high propriety acts and if there is no response,
Bares arms to force a response.

38:2 Therefore when the Tao is lost, there is virtue,
When virtue is lost, there is benevolence,
When benevolence is lost, there is righteousness,
When righteousness is lost, there are rites.
Rites are only the shell of faith and loyalty and the beginning of disorder.

Foreknowledge is only a flowery pretense of the Tao,
And the beginning of ignorance.

38:3 Therefore the sage dwells on what is real and not on the superficial,
Dwells on the fruit and not the flower,
Rejects one and accepts the other.

Paraphrase:
38:1 A person of great potential is unconscious of potential and therefore has pure potential. A person of lesser potential is always conscious of potential and therefore loses potential. The person of high potential does not consciously plan actions, depending instead on spontaneous knowledge of Tao process. A benevolent person acts in the interest of benevolence only. A righteous person acts in order to display righteousness. A person of high propriety acts. In the absence of a proper response the person of high propriety tries to force a response which meets his or her expectation.

38:2 When one moves away from the true and natural instincts of Tao process then comes moral rectitude. Out of moral rectitude comes a disposition to do good. Out of this benevolence one develops a sense of righteousness that is far removed from the natural rightness of Tao process. Finally righteousness degrades into hollow rites which are only the empty shell of natural rightness. Rites are the beginning of decay into disorder. Extensive knowledge of rites does not make one any closer to the Tao process. On the contrary, such knowledge is really ignorance.

38:3 Therefore the sage dwells on the underlying reality of Tao process and not on the superficiality of rites. Rejecting superficiality and accepting the real is like choosing the fruit and not the flower.

For Thought:
This chapter delineates the path that leads away from the Tao process to the current

state of humanity. Our society is now based on superficial, self-serving actions and on political manipulation. Ego and its associated greed have driven us to the brink of psychosis. All the things and actions which we are conditioned to believe will make us feel better about ourselves, do not do so. Thus we strive mightily to prop up a society that continues to collapse. The religious and philosphical systems to which we turn for personal direction and growth are also failing. Hollow ritual has supplanted meaningful presence. Bureaucracy has superseded ministry. Politics has buried principle. Propriety suppresses natural values. How may we regain the lost reality and restore ourselves to our original potency? How may we grow into our natural potential? By walking backward down the path.

For Action:
Start an active search for true, uncontaminated knowledge both within yourself and in the historical and philosophical record. Look behind your perceived values and philosophy. Where did they originate? Do you believe what you believe? Do you accept it because you were told to accept it? Peel away ritual and embellishments. Examine what you find at the center. Record this search in your journal.

Related Reading:

Section 38:1   Read 2:2, 3:3, 29:1, 43:2, 47:2, 48:1, 57:3, 64:3
Section 38:2   Read 18:1, 19 (all)
Section 38:3   Read 12:1, 12:2, 72:3

Reflections

_____

_____

_____

_____

_____

_____

_____

_____

_____

_____

_____

_____

_____

ON UNITY

39:1   These things from ancient times achieved unity:
         Heaven achieved it, and became clear,
         Earth achieved it, and became stable,
         Spirit achieved it, and became sanctified,
         The valley achieved it, and became full,
         Leaders achieved it, and became statesmen.
         All of this resulted from unity.
         Heaven without clarity would soon split apart.
         Earth without stability would soon quake.
         Spirit without sanctity would soon wither and die.
         The valley without fullness would soon run dry.
         Leaders without statesmanship would soon fall from power.

39:2   Therefore power is based on humility,
         The low is the foundation for the high.
         Because of this leaders call themselves alone, lonely, and unworthy.
         Does this not acknowledge humility as a base?

39:3   The value of a chariot depends on the unity of its pieces.
         Desire not to be as rare as jade,
         Rather be as firm and as strong as rocks.

Paraphrase:
39:1   There is an underlying unity to everything. It lends stability to nature, divinity
to spirit, and statesmanship to leaders. Denying or resisting this unity results in
destruction and decline.

39:2   True power comes from humility. By joining the masses, leaders are revered
and elevated. Because of this leaders associate themselves with the people. Thus they
acknowledge humility as a base for power.

39:3 The individual parts of a vehicle have no value as a vehicle until they are assem-
bled. The value is in the unity. Therefore do not seek to set yourself aside like a precious jewel in its case. Rather you should draw strength from your unity with the
bedrock of nature.

For Thought:
There is a growing body of evidence supporting the idea that humanity has one or at
most a few common origins. Disciplines as diverse as mythology, archaeology, paleoan-
thropology, and etymology are making inter-disciplinary connections which are too
compelling to dismiss as mere coincidence or parallel development. Further, it appears
that the Neaderthals were not crude louts and that some of their spiritual and religious
ideas have survived into modern times.

For Action:
Read Joseph Campbell's Masks of God series, especially the volume on primitive
mythology. Read Cities of Dreams by Stan Gooch.

Related Reading:
Section 39:1   Read 10:1, 22:2
Section 39:2   Read 42:3

RETURNING AND YIELDING

40:1   Returning is the motion of the Tao.
        Yielding is the function of the Tao.

40:2   All things come from being.
        Being comes from non-being.

Paraphrase:
40:1   The Tao is cyclical. It is a closed loop. Thus, wherever one is in the cycle, one's motion is returning to another part of the cycle. One's function is to yield to the flow of Tao process.

40:2   The cycle of Tao process is the coming forth of things to being and the ultimate return to non-being.

For Thought:
Section 40:2 helps to distinguish between non-being and nonexistence. The state of non-being is also the state of infinite creative power and potential. It is no-thing, but it is assuredly not nothing.

For Action:
Think about turning inward to visit your inner-self. Be very still and very quiet, first filtering out the noises around you, then filtering out the inner static of what Buddhists call the monkey mind. Visualize yourself walking through the buzzing cloud of vagrant thoughts, pulling aside a heavy curtain, and entering your own sanctum sanctorem. Return to your own center. Now listen to the noiseless no-thing. Listen for the flow of Tao process. When you sense it, join it. Yield to its flow backward down the path. Go with it to its origin and be one with all.

Related Reading:
Section 40:1   Read 16:1, 22:1, 28:1
Section 40:2   Read 1:3, 25:1

DILIGENT PRACTICE, HIDDEN REWARDS

41:1   The best person hears of the Tao and practices it diligently.
        The average person hears of the Tao and studies it sporadically.
        The base person hears of the Tao and laughs heartily at it.
        If it were not laughed at, it would not be the Tao.

41:2   Hence the proverbs:
        Enlightenment in the Tao seems to be dullness.
        Advancing in the Tao seems to be retreating.
        The smooth Tao seems uneven.
        High virtue seems low.
        Pure whiteness seems soiled.
        Great virtue seems insufficient.
        Solid virtue seems unsteady.
        Basic substance seems mutable.
        Vast space has no corners.
        The great vessel is completed slowly.
        Great music is hard to hear.
        Great form has no shape.

41:3   The Tao is hidden and nameless,
        Yet it nourishes and fulfills.

Paraphrase:
41:1   The wise student studies the Tao diligently. The mediocre student studies the
Tao sporadically. The foolish student fails to understand the subtlety of the Tao and
laughs at it. If the Tao were not laughed at by the foolish one, then it would not be the
Tao.

41:2   There are old proverbs which say:
Enlightenment in the Tao seems dull. Advancing seems to be going backward down the
path. Great potential is hidden. Nothing seems to be what it is. Understanding is difficult and slow coming. The form of Tao is amorphous.

41:3   Like the Tao itself, its rewards are hidden, but they sustain and fulfill.

For Thought:
We live in a world where we are taught to expect instant results in everything we do. We
also learn from an early age that technology will supply us with equipment, tapes, techniques, and a thousand other gadgets and gimmicks to make our instant results materi-
alize even faster. It is a small wonder that the idea of diligent long-term study which
produces non-flashy, intangible results is alien to our culture.

For Action:
Read one chapter of the Tao Te Ching each day. If you own more than one translation,
compare versions and think about the underlying truth which produced disparate
visions in the translators. Make notes in your journal.

Related Reading:
Section 41:1   Read 70 (all)
Section 41:2   Read 28:1, 45:1
Section 41:3   Read 35:2

ACHIEVING BALANCE

42:1   The Tao gave birth to one,
One gave birth to two,
Two gave birth to three,
Three gave birth to all things.

42:2   All things carry yin and embrace yang.
By blending these two breaths they achieve balance.

42:3   People hate to be alone, lonely, and unworthy,
Yet leaders describe themselves by these names.

42:4   Often gain is loss, and loss is gain.

42:5   I will teach what the ancients taught.
A violent man will die an unnatural death.
I will make this the basis of my teaching.

Paraphrase:
42:1   The Tao manifested itself as a unity, which in turn produced the duality of Yin and Yang. The duality produced a mediating principle. These three principles underly all the physical manifestations of the universe.

42:2   All things, animate and inanimate, have both Yin and Yang principles. A blending of these two principles produces natural balance.

42:3   People don't like thinking of themselves as being alone or unworthy. But leaders describe themselves this way.

42:4   Thus they acknowledge that they gain stature by losing stature and lose stature by gaining stature.

42:5   The ancients taught that violent people, because they lose the balance of Yin and Yang, die an unnatural death. This is the basis of Taoist teaching.

For Thought:
This chapter presents the important concept which has been called the great Taoist triad. From the original unity came the duality of Yin and Yang, the passive and active principles. From this duality came the principle of the life force, also called the vital breath, which acts as a mediating connecting principle for Yin and Yang. This mediating principle blends Yin and Yang and maintains a natural dynamic balance between the two. In human society these principles translate to the tripartite functions which have survived in some form from Paleolithic time to the present. The three functions in primitive society were the hunter-gatherers, the warriors, and the priests. The hunter-gatherers were bound to the earth and were expressions of the generative feminine Yin principle. The warriors were the sons of heaven and were expressions of the active, aggressive masculine Yang principle. Finally, the priests in the metaphysical realm mediated between heaven and earth. In the physical realm they functioned as leaders who mediated between the warriors and the hunter-gatherers. Societies in which the leaders and priests have abdicated the role of mediators, to form a collusion with the warrior function, have lost their natural balance and will lose their viability as a result.

For Action:
Is there a difference between duality, dualism, and polarity? Look the words up and record your thoughts on the differences. Consider the ideas that duality may express two complementary parts of a whole; that dualism may imply two irreducible elements in opposition; and that polarity may convey the notion of diametrically opposed, highly charged, and totally separated elements.

Related Reading:
Section 42:1   Read 1 (all)
Section 42:2   Read 28:1
Section 42:3   Read 39:2
Section 42:4   Read 7:2, 22:2
Section 42:5   Read 30:1, 30:2, 73 (all)   87

STILL AND QUIET

43:1   The softest thing in the universe can overcome the hardest thing.
        That which has no substance can penetrate where there is no space.

43:2   Thus I understand the value of action without deeds.
        Teaching without words and the value of action without deeds,
        Are attained by very few.

Paraphrase:
43:1   Just as water overcomes rock, so the softest things can overcome the hardest.
Likewise idea can penetrate substance.

43:2   By the same token great things can be accomplished with minimal action.
Great lessons can be taught with few words. Only a very few people understand these
things.

For Thought:
Your yielding feminine principle is powerful enough to overcome your over-developed
masculine principle. In doing so you can ultimately achieve balance and accord with the
Tao process. The effort is in the seeking. The bad news is that you have no choice but to
seek the mystical Tao in your own way. The good news is that seek and you will find it.

For Action:
The value of action without deeds and teaching with no talking is best found in and by
you. Sit very still and take action. Make no words with your mouth or your mind and
learn your own teaching. It is all inside you, but you have to be very still and very quiet
to find it.

Related Reading:
Section 43:1   Read 36:1, 40:1, 78:1
Section 43:2   Read 2:2, 37:1, 48:1, 56:2, 63:1

RICHES AND FAME,
SELF AND CONTENTMENT

44:1   Which is more important, fame or self?
Which is more valuable, self or wealth?
Which is more painful, profit or loss?
Strong desires lead to wasteful spending.
Excessive hoarding leads to heavy loss.
To know contentment, is to avoid disgrace.
To know when to stop, is to avoid danger.
Thus one can endure for a long time.

Paraphrase:
44:1   Would you rather be rich and famous or have a contented inner life? Which is more painful, worrying about profits or worrying about losses? Riches cause wasteful spending. Hoarding causes heavy loss. It is better to be content than to be disgraced by a squandered life. Stop before you incur the dangers of riches and fame. You will endure as a result.

For Thought:
A multimillionaire once said that to be rich you don't have to be smart. You just have to love money more than anything else. Lao Tzu teaches that the more you look outward for value and esteem, the less you have. A teacher more familiar to Westerners said, "Will a person gain anything if he wins the whole world but loses his life? To know self and to find contentment therein allows you to more realistically assess the value of riches and fame.

For Action:
Choose something you own and to which you have a degree of attachment. Pick something that you have put away or stored. Get it out and look at it. Evaluate it as objectively as you can. Why is it valuable to you? Do you use it or do you simply worry about where to keep it. Are you afraid that someone will steal it? Do you own it or does it own you? How would your life be altered if you gave it away or sold it? Would you suffer great loss or enjoy new freedom? Think about it.

Related Reading:
Section 44:1   Read 32:1, 46:2, 81:2

LOOKING BEHIND APPEARANCES

45.

45:1   Great perfection seems imperfect,
Yet it is never used up.
Great fullness seems empty,
Yet it is never exhausted.
Great straightness seems bent.
Great skill seems inept.
Great eloquence seems inarticulate.

45:2   Movement overcomes cold.
Stillness overcomes heat.

45:3   The sage, calm and still,
Is a model for the world.

Paraphrase:
45:1   There is a remarkable dichotomy between human standards and the true, correct working of the Tao process. Thus things that are in perfect attunement with the Tao process seem to be out of place or malfunctioning to us.

45:2   There is, however, a natural, constantly shifting balance in the world that is both dynamic in process and static in principle.

45:3   The sage knows the principle and thus finds a position at the stillpoint or center of the process. In doing so the sage becomes a model for everyone.

For Thought:
There is a commercial for dandruff shampoo which says, "You never get a second chance to make a first impression." This is true, but it has hidden in it a sad commentary on our interactions with others. The implication is that the first impression is the only one, superficial as it might be. Are we so alienated from one another that one flaw in appearance is enough to establish a person as unworthy of our consideration?

For Action:
Pick a person with whom you interact. Write a character sketch of this person. Include physical appearance, mode of dress, idiosyncrasies which you have noticed, and any other unique physical features of which you are aware. Now make a detailed description of this person's personality, mode of thinking, and emotional state. When you are finished ask yourself how much you really know about the person. How many of the things which you have written down are factual and how many are superficial? In future interactions try to communicate and to develop more meaningful insights about the person. Remember that one who does not trust enough will not be trusted.

Related Reading:
Section 45:1   Read 4:1, 6 (all), 35:2, 38:3, 41:2
Section 45:2   Read 26 (all), 42:2
Section 45:3   Read 15:2, 16:1

ACHIEVING CONTENTMENT

46.

46:1   When the world follows the Tao,
Race horses are used for draft animals.
When the world rejects the Tao,
War horses are raised in parks.

46:2   No crime is greater than greed.
No misery is greater than discontent.
No fault causes more sorrow than coveting goods.
Contentment with what one has is true contentment.

Paraphrase:
46:1   When the Tao process prevails in the world competitiveness declines. When the Tao process is subverted aggression is everywhere.

46:2   Greed is the greatest crime. Discontent causes the greatest misery. Constant wanting causes constant sorrow. Knowing that what one has is enough is true contentment.

For Thought:
How much of what we do in the world is done out of competitiveness and greed? How often does competition transform to naked aggression? Is this the only way that we can function as humans? I don't think so.

For Action:
Think about your work and your motivation for doing it. Be conscious of conflict in your work relationships. Direct your thoughts and passion toward the unfolding work process instead of toward competition with your coworkers. Make notes of your observations of competition and aggression in the workplace, both in yourself and others.

Related Reading:
Section 46:2   Read 33:2, 44 (all)

KNOWING ALL BY LOOKING INWARD

47:1   Without going outside,
         One can know the world.
         Without looking out the window,
         One can see the Tao.
         The farther one goes,
         The less one knows.

47:2   Therefore the sage:
         Knows without going out,
         Sees without looking,
         Achieves without doing.

Paraphrase:
47:1   One can know the world without going into it. One can know the Tao without
looking outside for it. The more one searches externally for meaning, the less one knows
of meaning.

47:2   Sages know by turning inward. They see by searching self. They accomplish
through awareness of process and not by deeds.

For Thought:
This chapter illustrates the difference between the analytical empiricism of the Western
scientist and the holistic awareness of the Taoist sage. The scientist rips things apart
searching for their most elementary particle and then tries to construct logical models
which mirror their form and function. The sage removes self and tries to reach an intuitive understanding of the intertwined parts of natural process by observing things functioning in the process.

For Action:
Practice introspection as often as possible. Do so by stilling the mind. Sweep aside
thoughts of external things. Don't look out the windows of your senses. Turn instead
and walk into the labyrinth of your mind. Walk toward the center. You will know the way
intuitively. When you arrive at the original, natural center of yourself you will discover
that it is also the center of the universe; no, truly it is the universe.

Related Reading:
Section 47:1   Read 48:1
Section 47:2   Read 43:2, 45:3, 48:2

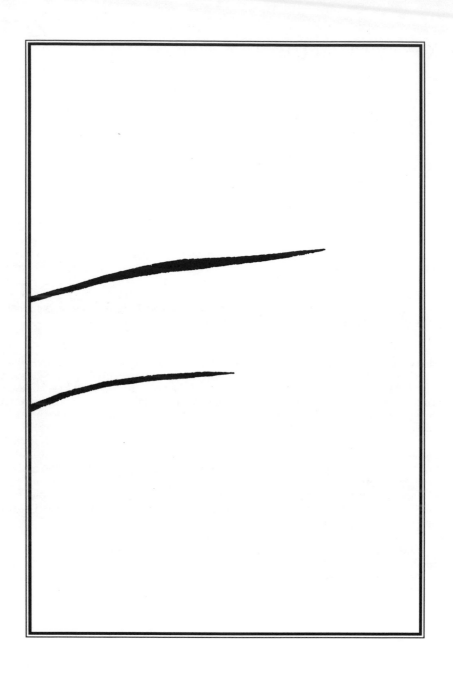

SIMPLIFY

48:1   In the pursuit of learning, one accumulates every day.
         In hearing the Tao, one simplifies every day.
         Simplify and simplify again,
         Until the state of action without deeds is achieved.
         Through action without deeds nothing is left undone.

48:2   One can win the world by leaving it alone.
         If one meddles in the world, he is unfit to win it.

Paraphrase:
48:1   In the pursuit of academic learning we stuff our minds with facts and figures. In hearing the Tao we simplify. By continuously simplifying we can achieve a state of deep understanding of underlying process. With this understanding we accomplish everything that needs doing with a minimum of action.

48:2   We can win over the world by letting the natural process run without interference. If we tamper with the world, we are unfit to win it over.

For Thought:
It has been said that American education trains us to use technology, but does not teach us to think. Thus, we become wise fools. We assume that everything should be organized to fit our technological conception of order. We think ourselves to be better at organizing nature than the nature from which we learned our skills.

For Action:
The Heisenberg Uncertainty Principle, in its most philosophical statement, says that you can't observe an event without altering it. Think of a situation in which you are involved. Think of ways in which you can allow events to unfold while minimizing your influence of the process. Do you know what laissez-faire means? Look it up. While you have the dictionary out, look up sophomoric.

Related Reading:
Section 48:1   Read 2:2, 43:2, 47 (all), 63 (all)
Section 48:2   Read 57:1, 57:3, 64:3

OPEN-MINDEDNESS, IMPARTIALITY

49:1 The sage is open-minded.
He adopts the mind of the people as his mind.

49:2 To those who are good, he is good.
To those who are not good, he is also good.
Thus he attains goodness.
Of those who trust, he is trusting.
Of those who do not trust, he is also trusting.
Thus he attains trust.

49:3 The sage merges harmoniously with the mind of the world.
People look to him and listen,
And the sage treats them as his children.

Paraphrase:
49:1 Sages do not prejudge or impose their opinions. They
truly listen to people and accept what they say as their view of truth.

49:2 They conduct themselves in the same manner with everyone, even those whom
they perceive to be bad in their actions. Thus they cultivate goodness in themselves and
in others. They display universal trust, even to those who do not trust in return. As a
result they cultivate trust in themselves and in others.

49:3 Sages are open-minded and impartial. Because they are so, people value their
opinion and judgement. Sages treat people as their children. They help without interfering or dominating.

For Thought:
This chapter doesn't imply that sages are mindless chameleons who change color to
suit their surroundings. Rather, it is that they recognize truth as a many faceted jewel.
Each of us looks at a particular facet. We describe truth as we see it there. Sages adopt
the mind of the people, knowing that there is an underlying truth which is the whole of
all individual perceptions. This universal truth is a manifestation of the Tao process.
Having discovered the truth underlying the mind of the people, and by tapping the Tao
process, sages act accordingly and consistently, no matter how others behave. By emulating sages, we can be proactive, following our own inner potential, instead of reactive
to constantly shifting external influence.

For Action:
Work at non-judgemental, unbiased listening for one full day. When someone explains
something to you or discusses a problem, avoid framing any reply until the speaker is
totally finished. Before framing a reply, repeat what the speaker said by paraphrasing
and summarizing key points. Listen for feedback and tweak your understanding until
you and the speaker agree exactly on what was said. Above all avoid the syndrome
which has been described by the statement, "Don't try to confuse me with the facts. My
mind is made up."

Related Reading:
Section 49:1   Read 7:2, 22:2
Section 49:2   Read 17:2, 27:2, 27:3, 63:2, 63:5, 79 (all)
Section 49:3   Read 5:1, 7:2, 45:3

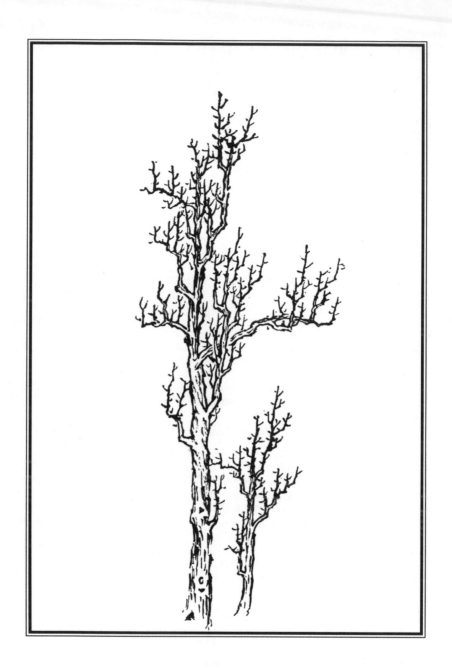

LIVING AND DYING

50:1   As life departs, death arrives.
        Three people in ten are followers of life.
        Three people in ten are followers of death.
        Three people in ten cling to life and follow death as a result.
        Why is this so?
        Because they strive excessively for life.
        One who knows how to live can walk in the hills without fear of
                rhinocerous or tiger.
        He can go into battle without being touched by weapons.
        The rhinocerous can find no place to thrust his horn.
        The tiger can find no place to clasp his claws.
        The weapon can find no place to penetrate.
        Why is this so?
        Because he has no room for death.

Paraphrase:
50:1   Life and death are a natural duality. Some people pursue life, some pursue death. Some pursue life so relentlessly that they kill themselves in the effort. But one who is balanced can walk into danger and, through focus and clarity, walk out unscathed. Why is this so? It is because this person knows underlying process and thus has no concern with life and death.

For Thought:
Almost all of us would say that we are followers of life. Think about where your life is, compared to where your attention and efforts are directed. Look inward to discover the well-spring of your life and to judge its quality. But so much of our efforts are directed to pulling life out of the senses. We tend to judge quality of life in terms of the degree to which we are able to garner sensual gratification. As a result we strive excessively for life and die outside.

For Action:
Set aside some definite period of time each day for examination and cultivation of your inner life. Use that time to study some spiritual or inspirational writing. Keep a journal with notes of your reading and contemplation. Use at least part of the time allotted for some form of meditation or prayer. Resolve that each day you will follow after life and recognize it in both the mundane events and the mystical process which unfold around you.

Related Reading:
Section 50:1   Read 16:2, 44 (all), 52 (all), 55:1, 59 (all), 75:3

BORN OF TAO, NOURISHED BY VIRTUE 51.

51:1   All things are born of the Tao.
        Virtue nourishes them.
        Nature forms them.
        Environment completes them.
        Thus all things revere the Tao and respect virtue.
        This is not done because of any mandate.
        It is done because it is natural.
        Therefore all things are born of the Tao and nourished by virtue.
        The Tao develops, cultivates, nourishes, shelters, comforts, and protects.

51:2   Bearing without possessing,
        Working without taking credit,
        Leading without dominating,
        This is the mystic virtue.

Paraphrase:
51:1   The Tao is the universal generative principle. All things come out of the Tao
and are imbued with potential. They take form in nature and are individualized by environment. Thus every manifestation of Tao is a tribute to the Tao process and to developing potential. Tao is the mother and potential is the nurse. The natural process works to
rear and nurture all things.

51:2   The natural Tao process works. It does so impartially and behind the scenes. It
is itself mystic potential.

For Thought:
In the West the universe is seen as a creation by an external father or masculine principle. In the East it is seen as a birth brought forth by a mother or feminine principle.

For Action:
The unfolding and development of your potential is a natural process which goes on for
your entire life. You are never too old to continue the process. If you abandon it and
become an inflexible, completed thing, you will be unhappy and discontented. Think
about yourself and write some areas of thought or study for which you feel that you have
some latent talent or interest. Pick one and study it for a while. If you lose interest, go
back to your list and work on another.

Related Reading:
Section 51:1   Read 25:1
Section 51:2   Read 2:2, 10:2, 34:1, 77:2

KNOWING PROCESS, LEARNING CONSTANCY

52:1   The universe had a beginning,
Which may be considered its mother.
By knowing the mother the sons can be understood.
Understand the sons, but keep to the mother,
And avoid harm throughout life.

52:2   Keep your mouth closed,
Guard your senses,
And life will be without toil.
Open your mouth,
Busy yourself in worldly affairs,
And there will be no hope in your life.

52:3   Seeing the small is insight.
Yielding is strength.
Use enlightenment, but return to insight,
And avoid misfortune.
This is practicing constancy.

Paraphrase:
52:1   The universe began in Tao process which thus may be considered its mother. By knowing underlying process we can understand the manifestations. Understanding manifestations is good, but don't forget underlying process. Doing so will help you to avoid harm throughout your life.

52:2   Don't talk too much. Don't become absorbed in your senses and your life will be easy and serene. If you talk all the time and meddle in people's affairs, you will find yourself in constant trouble.

52:3   Focus until you see the smallest details. This will give you insight. Yielding to the flow of things requires the strength to rise above ego. The enlightenment one experiences from knowing process is useful. But never forget to see details and develop insight. Thus you will avoid misfortune. You will learn constancy of purpose.

For Thought:
It has been said facetiously that an expert is someone who knows more and more about less and less until he or she knows everything about nothing. There may be a profound truth underlying the humor. As you become more and more knowledgeable about a subject you are able to see through the veil of superficial detail to the invisible underlying process. To a casual observer your enlightenment may appear to be knowing everything about nothing.

For Action:
Resolve to become an expert in something. Pick a process in your work or one which interests you as an avocation. See how much you can find out about the process which you have chosen. Can you find people who are experts themselves? How many books are there about your chosen topic. Make notes on the smallest details which you encounter. Stay focused on the process which you have chosen. Do this for six months then evaluate your understanding and whether you want to continue your study of the process you originally chose. If not, choose another and begin again.

Related Reading:
Section 52:1   Read 1:2, 6:1
Section 52:2   Read 16:1, 29:1, 56:1, 56:2
Section 52:3   Read 16:2, 22:1, 55:2

DEVIATING FROM THE TAO

53.

53:1   If I had a little knowledge, I would follow the great Tao,
       And fear only that I would deviate from it.
       The great Tao is broad and plain,
       But people prefer the side paths.

53:2   The courts are magnificent.
       The fields are barren,
       And the graineries are empty.
       Officials wear embroidered clothes,
       Carry double edged swords,
       And satiate themselves on food and drink.
       They accumulate excessive wealth.
       This is called thievery.
       It is far from the Tao.

Paraphrase:
53:1   With only a little insight one can recognize the value of following the Tao
process. The path of Tao is natural and easy to follow, but people prefer their own agendas.

53:2   A good example of this is politicians and bureaucrats who live and work in
magnificent surroundings while common people starve. They own fine things, eat and
drink only the best, and accumulate large amounts of money. This is thievery and is far
removed from the natural rightness of the Tao.

For Thought:
The world can be the source of both profound understanding of the underlying Tao
process and an unending supply of distractions.

For Action:
Think about the way your life is going. Ask yourself why you have the things you have. Is
it because you truly need these things? Is it because you need to impress other people?
Or is it because someone convinced you that you needed what you have? How could
you simplify your life? Write down where you are, compared to where you yourself would
like to be.

Related Reading:
Section 53:1   Read 25:2, 41:1, 41:2, 70 (all)
Section 53:2   Read 75:1, 77:1

CULTIVATION OF VIRTUE

54:1   What is firmly placed cannot be uprooted.
       What is firmly embraced cannot escape.
       Because of these characteristics your sons and grandsons will honor you forever.

54:2   Cultivate virtue in yourself and it becomes real.
       Cultivate virtue in the family and it grows.
       Cultivate virtue in the community and it endures.
       Cultivate virtue in the country and it abounds.
       Cultivate virtue in the world and it becomes widespread.
54:3   Therefore measure individuals against yourself.
       Measure families against your family.
       Measure communities against your community.
       Measure countries against your country.
       Measure worlds against your world.
       How do I know the world?
       Because of this.

Paraphrase:
54:1   If you are steadfast in your pursuit of understanding, you will be remembered.

54:2   Cultivate your potential and it will grow to fruition. Your natural power will
spread through your family, your community, your country, and will become universal.

54:3   Measure other people's cultivation of potential against your own. Likewise do
so for families, communities, and nations. Tracing a path outwards from the rightness in
yourself will let you intuitively see the rightness in the world.

For Thought:
If you cultivate your natural potential and try to understand it through introspection,
you will grow as a person. Excellence shows in, and spreads from those who have it. But
it must start somewhere. It is up to you.

For Action:
Pick some event which occurred around you recently. Describe it and relate it to whatever process it manifested. Do you think that there was a rightness or wrongness about it?
Why?

Related Reading:
Section 54:1   Read 27:1
Section 54:2   Read 21:2

INFANT NATURE, NATURAL CHILD

55:1   He who has abundant virtue is like an infant.
        Poisonous creatures will not sting him.
        Wild beasts will not seize him.
        Birds of prey will not attack him.
        His bones are soft, his sinews weak, but his grasp is strong.
        He has not known a woman, yet he is aroused,
        Because his virility is at a peak.
        He can scream all day without becoming hoarse,
        Because his harmony is perfect.

55:2   Knowing harmony, is knowing constancy.
        Knowing constancy, is enlightenment.

55:3   To enhance one's vitality causes confusion.
        To control one's breath invites disaster.
        To develop excessive strength hastens decay.
        This is contrary to the Tao.
        Things contrary to the Tao soon perish.

Paraphrase:
55:1   The person with abundant potential is like an infant. Because of his or her innocence, danger seems to stay away. The infant's body is not fully developed but its instincts
and potential are. It can do what is natural to it without discomfort. This is because there
is perfect harmony between the natural child and its surroundings.

55:2   Knowing such harmony gives one constancy of purpose in developing one's
potential. Recognition of one's true nature and potential is enlightenment.

55:3   Trying to artificially form oneself into some mold causes a muddled mind. Trying
to impose one's will on one's body causes disasterous results. Trying to be bigger and
stronger than anyone else quickly leads to decay. These activities are all deviations from
natural Tao process. Such deviations will lead to one's downfall.

For Thought:
The word infant comes from Latin roots which literally mean one who is unable to speak.
A person who never learned to speak, verbalize, or intellectualize would live and interact
with his or her environment in a much different way than we do. There would be an inner
harmony between logic and intuition since, without language, linear logic could not domi-
nate the thinking process. Without language one would be able to tap into and use the
racial memory hidden in, or driven to the subconscious. Thus one would be a natural child
with no learned behavior and with complete harmony with one's surroundings.

For Action:
Visualize yourself as an infant who has not learned to speak. Go through your day trying to
perceive and react to things and people with childlike interest and innocence. Avoid ver-
balizing your reactions to the input to your senses. For example, if you look at and touch
an orange, don't say to yourself, this is an orange. It is orange-yellow in color and textured
to the touch. Instead look at it closely and perceive its color. Feel of it and think about the
feel that it has on your fingers. Smell of it. Toss it into the air and feel its mass when you
catch it. Don't intellectualize it, experience it. Do this with as many things as you can
through a day.

Related Reading:
Section 55:1   Read 10:1, 20:3, 50:1
Section 55:2   Read 16 (all), 52:3
Section 55:3   Read 30:2

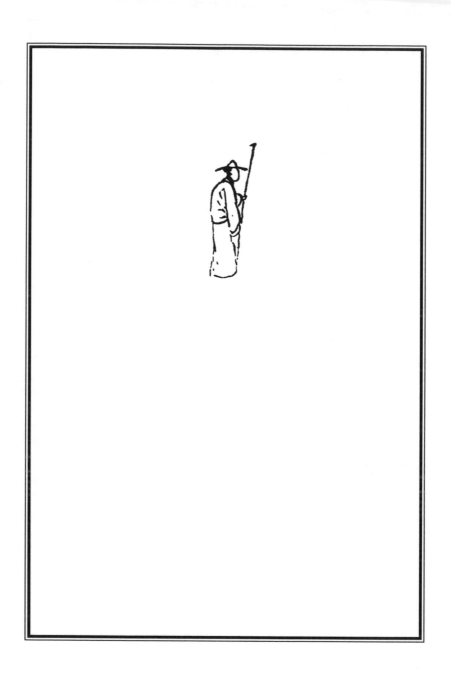

THE MAKING OF A MYSTIC

56:1   He who knows does not talk.
       He who talks does not know.

56:2   Keep your mouth closed,
       Guard your senses,
       Mute the glare,
       Combine with dust.
       Blunt the sharpness,
       Untangle the knots,
       This is called mystic unity.

56:3   He who has attained mystic unity is beyond love and hate,
       Beyond profit and loss,
       Beyond honor and disgrace.
       Therefore he is honored by all.

Paraphrase:
56:1   The more one relies on intellectual verbalization the less one knows intuitively.

56:2   Don't rely on verbalization. Avoid the distractions of the senses. Don't think of
yourself as brightly shining. Instead try to merge with the collective unconsciousness.
Curb your cutting wit and incisive knowledge. Go deep inside yourself and untangle the
knotty confusion which plagues you. Thus you will achieve primal union and act as an
integrated, whole person.

56:3   When you achieve primal union you will move beyond concern for superficial
distinctions. Whether people love you or hate you, whether you gain or lose, whether
you are honored or reviled will not be of concern to you. Because you are not concerned
with worldly pettiness, you will be honored by all.

For Thought:
By looking inward you can discover your true nature and potential, which is also the true
nature of all people. By recognizing the ancient feminine principle, as well as the masculine principle, you can achieve a primal union within yourself. You can heal the self-
inflicted wounds caused by repression of one aspect of your selfhood and by domination by the other. When you achieve primal union you will become a mystic in the
purest sense of the word.

For Action:
Have you ever worried about what people will think? Have you ever thought about snap-
py comebacks or putdowns? Have you ever been more concerned with how smart you
appeared to be in a meeting than you were with the substance of your presentation? In
your work and actions today remove the "big I" of your own ego. The "big I" distorts the
natural flow of Tao process around you and interferes with your efficiency and effectiveness as a person.

Related Reading:
Section 56:1   Read 5:3, 81:1
Section 56:2   Read 1:3, 4:2, 52:2
Section 56:3   Read 79:2, 79:3

115

LOSS IN DISORDER, GAIN IN NONACTION

57:1   Govern a country with justice.
Wage war with surprise tactics.
Win the world by leaving it alone.

57:2   How do I know this is so?
By this:
The more restrictions there are,
The poorer people become.
The more weapons there are,
The more disordered the nation becomes.
The more knowledge and skill there are,
The more strange novelties appear.
The more laws and regulations there are,
The more thieves appear.

57:3   Therefore the sage says:
I take no action and the people reform,
I love quiet and the people become upright,
I do not meddle and the people prosper,
I desire not to desire and the people simplify their lives.

Paraphrase:
57:1   A country can be ruled with justice and war can be won with clever strategy, but the only way to win over the world is by leaving it alone.

57:2   This is illustrated by the course of events. The more regulations and rules there are, the more impoverished people become. The more weapons there are, the more disorder reigns in the streets. The more we value technology, the more gimmicks and trivial inventions we have. The more laws there are, the more outlaws will break or circumvent them.

57:3   Sages, on the other hand, do not act and people reform naturally. They are quiet and people stop resisting and return to a natural honesty. Sages do not meddle in business or economics and people prosper. They simplify their lives by minimizing desires, and people follow their lead.

For Thought:
This chapter illustrates the wrong way and the right way to lead. The wrong way involves more and more laws, rules, and regulations. People are faced with the choice of becoming poor or becoming outlaws. Power and might become the rulers and weapons are used to enforce rule. Technology becomes the ultimate tool to enforce our will on both others and our surroundings. This is not the natural way and is a deviation from Tao process.

For Action:
Think about times that rules have been imposed on you which you considered arbitrary and unfair. For example, have you ever had a work rule such as a dress code or policy concerning telephones or copy machines? Did anyone violate the rules? Pick one example and write down a brief description of the rule and the response it caused. Now write down in a few words how you think it could have been handled. Think of ways which would achieve the desired result while causing a minimum of ill-will and resistance.

Related Reading:
Section 57:1   Read 29:1, 48:2, 60:1, 68 (all), 69 (all)
Section 57:2   Read 19 (all), 58:1, 72:1, 75 (all), 80 (all)
Section 57:3   Read 3:3, 37 (all), 64:5, 72:2

ACTION AND REACTION

58.

58:1   When government is not demanding,
         People are simple and honest.
         When government is demanding,
         The state is cunning and deceitful.

58:2   Happiness depends on misery.
         Misery hides beneath happiness.
         Where will it end?
         There is no order.
         Order becomes clever strategy.
         Good becomes evil.
         Thus people have been deluded for a long time.

58:3   Therefore be square without cutting,
         Be sharp, but not stabbing,
         Be straightforward, but not arrogant,
         Be bright, but not dazzling.

Paraphrase:
58:1   When government is done as a service, people are honest and straightforward
in their dealings. When the government demands its due and writes laws to support its
demands, there are always those who find loopholes in the laws.

58:2   The Taoist duality applies to happiness and misery. How can we know happiness if we don't know misery? The most miserable people are those who have fallen
from happiness. When will this confusion end? Order is turned into self-serving strategy.
Natural good is manipulated into evil. It's no wonder people are confused.

58:3   So be four-square in your dealings without cutting people down. Go to the heart
of matters but have a heart. Be direct but not arrogant. Be brilliant but hide your light.

For Thought:
Sometimes it is very easy to do the right thing for the wrong reason. What might start as
putting order and control into a process, may end up as a mechanism for self-aggrandis-
ement. Effective leadership can easily degrade into political expediency. Remember the
old saying: the road to hell is paved with good intentions.

For Action:
Think about your work and dealings with your co-workers. Consider both superiors and
subordinates. Review actions you have taken, decisions you have made, and goals you
have set. Are your actions, decisions, and goals all directed at product or service? Did
you do anything in your most recent workday which was more self-serving than process
enhancing?

Related Reading:
Section 58:1   Read 17 (all), 53:2, 57:2
Section 58:2   Read 3:3, 38:2, 65:2
Section 58:3   Read 22:2

MODERATION

59:1   In leading people and serving heaven,
There is nothing like moderation.
Through moderation one can submit early on.
By submitting early on one accumulates virtue.
By accumulating virtue one can overcome anything.
By overcoming all difficulties one knows no limits.
By knowing no limits one can be a leader.
If one holds to the mother principle of leadership, one will endure.
One will have deep roots and a firm basis.
This is the Tao of a long life and lasting vision.

Paraphrase:
59:1   Those who are moderate in their views and conduct will not find themselves taking dogmatic and untenable positions. By submitting to the natural flow of the Tao process they will develop their potential. With developed potential they can overcome anything. With boundless capability they can easily be leaders. As leaders, they should accentuate the yielding feminine principle rather than the dominating masculine principle. In doing so they will endure. By having a firm basis in the Tao process they will have long tenure as leaders and their leadership vision will endure after they are gone.

For Thought:
The moderate person is flexible enough to keep an open mind and not be a prisoner of dogma. Such a person can examine ideas both logically and intuitively without prejudice. This enables one to yield when necessary and to overcome all obstacles. The ability to yield comes from being firmly rooted in the Tao process.

For Action:
Today be particularly conscious of your reactions and thoughts as events unfold around you. Keep notes, especially regarding events, things, or people that evoke strong feelings in you. Consciously moderate your behavior and evaluate the underlying reasons for strong reactions. It's not necessary to compromise your principles. Just try to dissipate groundless, ego-based dogma.

Related Reading:
Section 59:1   Read 16:2, 29:3, 33 (all), 52 (all)

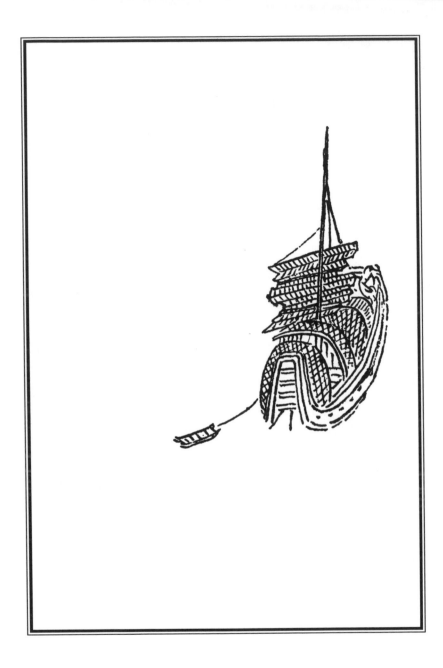

AVOID TAMPERING, ALLOW TAO

60:1 Ruling a country is like cooking a small fish.

60:2 When Tao is present in a country, evil spirits lose their power.
Not that they are powerless,
But that they do not harm people.
Not only do evil spirits not harm people,
But also the sage does not harm people.
Since neither does harm,
Virtue is accumulated in both.

Paraphrase:
60:1 In managing process the more you tamper, the more you disrupt.

60:2 When natural Tao process prevails, evil becomes ineffectual. It is not that evil is powerless. It is that people, by their attitude, render it impotent. In addition to this, people also do not allow erudite intelligence to harm them. Since neither does harm, people develop their full potential.

For Thought:
Our culture encourages and rewards initiative and individualism. These traits pay off in creativity, but they sometimes backfire. We assume that we know more than anyone about how to make things work. As a result we sometimes force changes in a process which doesn't need to be changed. We forget the advice, don't fix it if it isn't broke. This ill-advised, ego-driven tweaking is not beneficial. It is tampering.

For Action:
In your interactions with people today avoid tampering or meddling with relationships. Instead, concentrate on the process unfolding before you. Don't push, pull, or force responses. Don't interject your ego. If you perceive malevolent spirit in yourself or others, recognize it but don't allow it to affect you. Do the same for those who would manipulate you with superior knowledge. See if this approach causes a natural flow and growth in your relationships.

Related Reading:
Section 60:1   Read 48:2, 57 (all), 59 (all), 66:1
Section 60:2   Read 66:2, 66:3

COMPLEMENTARY SUBMISSION

61:1   A large country is like the female of the world.
        It is like the delta of a river.

61:2   The female overcomes the male by submission.
        She places herself beneath him.

61:3   By quietude and humility a large state can win over a small state.
        Through submission the small state is taken over by a large state.
        Thus one annexes by lowering itself,
        The other is annexed by staying low.
        The large state needs more people to support,
        The small state needs to serve.
        Both can get what they want,
        If the large country will humbly yield.

Paraphrase:
61:1   People and things tend to flow into a large country like water flowing through a river delta. People and things flow out of a large country so that it is generative like a female.

61:2   Through soft yielding a woman can overcome the aggressive hardness of a man.

61:3   By the same token a large country, through humble service, can win over a small state. By submitting, a small state can be absorbed into a large country. Thus both can achieve their goals by submitting and can complement each other thereby. It all begins with submission.

For Thought:
As I write this the news is full of the events taking place as the old Soviet Union crumbles and the independent republics emerge from the rubble. Now, instead of headlines about the Cold War and potential nuclear destruction, we read about mutual cooperation, aid, and partnership. Which sounds better?

For Action:
Pick an interaction or relationship which you have with someone either personal or professional. Choose one in which there is conflict or tension. What motivates your actions in the relationship? Write down feelings, thoughts, and anything else which is pertinent. Now put yourself in the other person's situation. Think about his or her experience, emotions, education, and so on. Imagine how he or she might think or feel while interacting with you. Write down your perceptions of the other person's feelings and thoughts in a column opposite your own. Now consider how you could submit in areas where there is tension or conflict. How can you complement each other's actions so that you both achieve your goals?

Related Reading:
Section 61:1   Read 7:2, 34:1, 66:1
Section 61:2   Read 10 (all)
Section 61:3   Read 66:2, 67:2, 76:2

ADVANCING IN THE TAO

62:1   All things tend toward the Tao.
        It is a good man's treasure and a bad man's protection.

62:2   Fine words can be sold,
        Good deeds can be offered as gifts.
        If a man errs in this manner, why reject him?

62:3   Therefore when the head of state is enthroned,
        Or the three ministers installed,
        Rather than to send a gift of jade or a team of four horses,
        It is better to sit and advance in the Tao.

62:4   Why was the Tao treasured by the ancients?
        Because those who seek will find it,
        And those who err will not be faulted.
        Therefore it is the greatest treasure.

Paraphrase:
62:1   Because of its value to all, the Tao is treasured.

62:2   People who are caught up in the superficialities of the world might buy and sell fine words or offer good works as gifts. But why should we reject those who make the error of not pursuing the Tao?

62:3   It is better to advance in the Tao than to present leaders with superficialities.

62:4   The ancients recognized the value of the Tao process. It is because those who seek the Tao process will find it. On the other hand, there is no fault in the error of not seeking the Tao. There is only loss. This makes the Tao an even greater treasure.

For Thought:
There is a natural tendency to avoid those with whom we don't agree and to out and out reject those whom we perceive as bad. But often our perception of bad means only that there is a conflict in basic interests or beliefs between ourselves and the bad person.

For Action:
Single out someone with whom you have contact and whom you perceive as uninformed, uncooperative, or self-serving. Identify the exact situations and events which caused you to develop this perception. How might you ease tension and resolve the conflict? Are there both teaching and learning opportunities for you in the situation?

Related Reading:
Section 62:1   Read 42:2
Section 62:2   Read 27:2
Section 62:4   Read 27:3, 49:2

SIMPLE ACTIONS ADD UP

63:1   Act without deeds, serve without doing.
        Taste the flavorless.

63:2   Whether great, small, many or few,
        Repay harsh deeds with virtue.

63:3   Deal with difficult things with simple acts.
        Deal with big things while they are small.
        Difficult tasks have easy beginnings.
        Large undertakings begin as small actions.

63:4   Therefore the sage never tries to do great things,
        And thus achieves greatness.

63:5   One who makes promises lightly will not be trusted.
        One who thinks things are easy will encounter great difficulty.
        Therefore the sage considers things difficult,
        And encounters no great difficulty.

Paraphrase:
63:1   The best effort is effortless. Do what you have to do without laboring mightily.

63:2   Deal with the harshness in your life with your potential instead of your sense of
right and wrong.

63:3   The most complex project can be successfully completed with simple actions.
Plan small, simple, individual steps which take you toward your objective. If you do so,
each step will be easy but, on a grand scale, you will accomplish difficult tasks. Many
small steps accumulate to form a large undertaking.

63:4   Because the sage never tries to do great things in a single step, he achieves
great things.

63:5   If you promise results without understanding process, you will fail to deliver
and will not be trusted. If you assume a project is easy, you will be surprised at its difficulty. If you consider everything to be difficult, you will not be surprised at the difficulty
which you do encounter.

For Thought:
The next chapter delineates the management cycle. This chapter reminds us that plans
must be followed by actions. Nothing will happen until you take the first step. The second step will seem easier and all the steps together will add up to monumental progress
toward the goal.

For Action:
Mentally prepare yourself for the next time someone does something which you consider
to be a harsh deed. Before responding to the action remove yourself from the situation
to the point that you don't take it personally. Respond impartially and dispassionately.
Search for the process which led to the deed. How can you use the natural flow of events
to achieve your own goals?

Related Reading:
Section 63:1   Read 2:2, 3:2, 35:1, 37:1, 43:2, 48:1
Section 63:2   Read 49:2, 62:4
Section 63:4   Read 34:1
Read all of Chapter 64.

SMALL BEGINNINGS, SUCCESSFUL ENDINGS

64:1   It is easy to hold what is still.
It is easy to plan for what has not begun.
Brittle things are easy to break.
Tiny things are easy to disperse.
Deal with things before they begin.
Establish order before disorder sets in.

64:2   A tree as big as an arm's breadth,
Begins as a small shoot.
A terrace nine tiers high,
Begins as a handful of dirt.
An ascent to high places,
Begins beneath one's feet.

64:3   Acting results in failure,
Grasping results in loss.
Therefore the sage does not act, hence does not fail.
He does not grasp, hence does not lose.

64:4   In their affairs people often fail while on the brink of success.
Therefore pay as much attention at the end as at the beginning,
And there will be no failure.

64:5   Therefore the sage desires not to desire.
He does not treasure rare goods,
He learns without learning,
And returns to the basics that men have lost.
He could assist all things in their natural flow,
Yet dares not interfere.

Paraphrase:
64:1   Processes which are firmly based in the natural order of things are easy to plan and control. Problems are easier to deal with early on. It is easier to maintain order than to reestablish it.

64:2   We can look at processes in the real world to see that even the biggest tree started from a sprout. Broadly terraced fields began with a handful of dirt. The longest journey began with one step.

64:3   We must recognize, however, that these processes proceed at a natural and reasonable pace. If we push hard to accelerate things, we introduce errors, omissions, and produce failure. If we grasp for results, we will suffer loss. It is better to go with the flow, than to drive toward the goal. It is better to take gains as they come, than to constantly grab for results.

64:4   Because they are impatient, people often fail when they are on the brink of success. If they devote as much attention and energy to the end of a project as to the beginning, they will always succeed.

64:5   Therefore focus on the work at hand, not on the reward. Learn by watching and participating in the process not just by studying reports, charts, memos, or books. When you have an understanding of the basic functioning of the process, you can expedite its flow without tampering or interfering.

For Thought:
This chapter is an overview of modern management practice. The management cycle can be remembered with the acronym, PACE, which stands for plan-act-control-evaluate. Most people lay plans for projects and act. However, many people fail to control and evaluate their actions by making sure that they really are going according to plan. They become impatient and take shortcuts which lead them away from their goal instead of toward it.

For Action:
Plan a personal or work project. Write down what you want to achieve. Think about the process which you are going to set in motion. Record the steps which will be required in the order in which they will have to be done. Then act on the plan. Record your progress, step by step. Refer to the plan to assure that you are really headed toward the goal. Evaluate progress and adjust your actions if you drift away from the goal. When you are finished, evaluate your accomplishment, decide on the next goal, and start again. PACE by PACE walk the thousand mile journey.

Related Reading:
Section 64:3   Read 24:1
Section 64:5   Read 3:1, 12:1
Read all of Chapter 63.

Reflections

_____

_____

_____

_____

_____

_____

_____

_____

_____

_____

_____

_____

_____

_____

_____

CLEVERNESS VERSUS SIMPLICITY

65:1   The ancients who practiced the Tao,
       Did not use it to increase the people's cleverness.
       Rather they kept the people simple.
       People who are cunning are difficult to govern.

65:2   Therefore he who governs with cleverness,
       Is like a bandit to the state.
       He who governs with simplicity,
       Is a boon to the state.
       These two are like standards.
       To always know these standards,
       Is to possess mystic virtue.
       Virtue becomes profound and far-reaching,
       And with all things returns to primal unity.

Paraphrase:
65:1   The ancient masters of Tao did not use it to make people clever. Instead they
preserved the people's uncomplicated original nature. When people are cunning they
are difficult to lead.

65:2   Those who lead people with clever strategy are like bandits. Those who lead
with simplicity are a boon to those who follow. These two modes are benchmarks of
good and bad leadership. To know these standards is an expression of mystic potential. Mystic potentialbecomes profound and far-reaching. It ultimately culminates in
primal unity.

For Thought:
Chuang Tzu said that men strive after what they do not know, but do not strive after
what they already know. Thus we consume knowledge with an insatiable appetite while
understanding withers. If you think that this is an alien concept in the Western world,
consider what got Adam and Eve evicted from the Garden of Eden.

For Action:
Clever strategies elicit cunning responses. In your dealings with others avoid complexity
in your approach. Be totally straightforward. If you sense yourself lapsing into con-
trivances or schemes to get over someone, stop. Be as honest as you can and consider
the results. Remember that the Taoist sage goes last and is soon placed first. Being can-
did does not automatically mean being brutal.

Related Reading:
Section 65:1   Read 3:2, 18 (all)
Section 65:2   Read 19 (all), 48:2

HUMILITY AND NON-CONTENTION

66:1   Rivers and seas are kings of the hundred valleys,
       Because they are skilled at staying low.
       That is why they are kings of the hundred valleys.

66:2   Therefore, to rise above the people,
       The sage by his words stays low.
       To lead the people,
       He places himself behind.

66:3   Thus the sage leads the people,
       Without them feeling oppressed.
       He stands before the people,
       Without doing them harm,
       And the world supports him tirelessly.

66:4   Because he does not compete,
       No one can compete with him.

Paraphrase:
66:1   Rivers and seas, because they are lower, receive everything valleys have
to offer.

66:2   Therefore develop true humility and non-contention in order to lead
the people.

66:3   Sages lead without oppression. They stand before their followers and do them
no harm. Because of these things, they are universally supported.

66:4   They do not compete, so no one can compete with them.

For Thought:
Just as we should seek a balance between the active and passive principles within ourselves, so also should we seek balance in our dealings with others. In primitive society
there are often just three functions: warriors, hunter- gatherers, and priests. The priestly
function is to mediate and arbitrate the interactions between the warriors and the
hunter-gatherers. In the ideal society, the priestly mediators successfully balance the
aggressive and oppressive action of the warriors and the passive and humble actions of
the hunter-gatherers. To survive in the modern world we must do the same.

For Action:
In your interactions with people around you, be aware of the roles you are taking on.
Are you being an argumentative and oppressive warrior? Or are you being a passive and
accomodating gatherer of the fruits of the earth? Consciously adopt the priestly role.
Step back from your interactions and find ways to mediate and accomodate both the
active and passive principles in your interactions. Both have great value when properly
balanced.

Related Reading:
Section 66:1   Read 8:1, 32:2, 61:1
Section 66:2   Read 7:2, 34:1, 39:2, 61:2, 68 (all), 81:2
Section 66:3   Read 60:2, 72:2, 81:3
Section 66:4   Read 8:3, 22:2

THREE TREASURES

67.

67:1   All people say that I am great, but different.
        Because I am different, I can be great.
        If I were not different, I would have become insignificant long ago.

67:2   I have three treasures which I cherish and keep;
        The first is compassion,
        The second is frugality,
        The third is not daring to go first in the world.
        With compassion, one can be courageous.
        With frugality, one can be generous.
        With humility, one can be a leader of those who complete things.
        If one is courageous without compassion,
        If one is generous without frugality,
        If one takes the lead without humility,
        Then death is sure to follow.

67:3   If one is compassionate in battle, victory will follow.
        If one is compassionate in defense, he will stand firm.
        Heaven protects its leaders by giving them compassion.

Paraphrase:
67:1   To be great is to be different. If you are the same as everyone else, then you will be hard pressed to rise above mediocrity.

67:2   The three treasures of the Taoist sage are compassion, frugality, and humility. Compassion breeds courage; frugality leads to generosity; going behind will put one in the forefront. Without compassion, courage becomes bravado. Without frugality and moderation, one will have nothing to give. Without humility, a leader is soon overthrown.

67:3   Those who temper competitiveness with compassion, will win a greater victory. Those who defend with compassion instead of vindictiveness, will be successful. A yielding softness protects followers of the Tao process.

For Thought:
Daring to be great, requires daring to be different. The people of the world are beginning to recognize the falseness and superficiality of leaders who fight for political gain and not for cause; who give away what is not theirs to give; who trumpet their greatness as leaders when they want to rule, but not to serve.

For Action:
Think of someone with whom you have recently been in conflict and with whom you have gained the upper hand. How can you extend a compassionate gesture without compromising your principles and without seeming to be condescending?

Related Reading:
Section 67:1   Read 20:3, 70:2
Section 67:2   Read 7:2, 34 (all), 39:2, 59 (all), 66 (all)
Section 67:3   Read 31 (all), 61:3, 69:3

139

TAKING CARE OF BUSINESS

68:1   The best soldier is not warlike.
          The best fighter does not lose his temper.
          The greatest victor does not join the battle.
          The greatest employer of men leads with humility.
          This is called the virtue of not contending.
          This is called the power of using others.
          This is called following heaven,
          The ultimate goal of the ancients.

Paraphrase:
68:1   In competition those who do best do not take things personally. They maintain focus on the competition and not on their opponents. In doing so they do not show off or lose their temper. Thus the best leaders remove ego from their work and lead by serving. This non-contentious approach allows them to develop their potentiality and empowers others to do so also. This is tapping the Tao process, the goal of the ancient masters.

For Thought:
Even in the ultimate competition, combat, Taoist sages maintain a distance from what they are doing. They remove ego and involvement of self from the conflict and by doing so are able to control the flow of the process which is going on around them.

For Action:
The next time you are experiencing a conflict with someone remember this chapter. Take an uninvolved interest in the flow of events. Instead of wading into the fray like a berserker, stand outside the conflict as if you were a third party watching it.

Related Reading:
Section 68:1   Read 8:3, 22:2, 66 (all), 67:2, 67:3

AVOIDING THE FIGHT, WINNING THE WAR

69:1   Soldiers have a saying which goes:
        Dare not be the host, rather be the guest;
        Dare not advance an inch, rather retreat a foot.

69:2   This is known as marching without a formation,
        Rolling up one's sleeves without showing arms,
        Making war with no weapons,
        Moving forward where there is no resistance.

69:3   There is no greater misfortune than not having a rival.
        By believing I have no rival I come close to losing my treasures.
        When evenly matched rivals make war,
        The side which does so with sorrow will win.

Paraphrase:
69:1   In conflict it is better not to be the aggressor, rather be the defender. Rather than advancing into a fight, it is better to let your opponent overextend and lose balance.

69:2   This is the guiding principle of guerilla warfare. The army can't be seen. The weapons are hidden. The advances come at points of weakness.

69:3   It is a great misfortune to believe that your rivals are non-existent and that your force is invincible. To do so will cause you to lose your compassion, frugality, and humility in leadership. It is better to fight with sorrow than with blood-lust. The one who fights with sorrow will ultimately prevail.

For Thought:
These days we are continually bombarded with messages designed to promote aggression. We have presidents who pride themselves in kicking ass. People who are sorrowful about loss of life and destruction of nature in war are branded wimps or non-patriotic. We rationalize our actions by directing our wars toward bullies and dictators. But if we punish enough bullies, we are in danger of becoming super-bullies. So victory in war should be celebrated like a funeral. Kicking ass should be a cause for sorrow that it was necessary, not a source of national pride.

For Action:
The actions of a nation are nothing more than the manifestations of the collective actions of its citizens. Carefully consider your actions the next time you sense conflict developing with someone. Instead of kicking ass and taking names, yield to the frontal assault. Examine the causes and process underlying the attack. Find areas within the conflict where you and your opponent can agree. Build from those areas of no resistance. Even if your opponent is overextended and off-balance from his or her attack, conduct yourself with compassion, and frugality in defense, and humility in leadership.

Related Reading:
Section 69:1   Read 15:1
Section 69:2   Read 30:1, 31 (all), 38:1, 68 (all)
Section 69:3   Read 22:2, 67:2, 67:3, 76:2

THE JEWEL IN YOUR HEART

70:1   My words are easy to understand and to put to practice,
         Yet no one in the world seems able to understand and to practice them.

70:2   My words have an ancient origin and my deeds have discipline.
         Because people fail to understand this,
         They do not understand me.
         Those who understand me are few.
         Thus I have great value.
         Therefore the sage wears coarse cloth,
         And carries precious jade in his heart.

Paraphrase:
70:1   The Tao process is easy to find and easy to practice. Because it is not flashy,
loud, or trendy, people are distracted and have great difficulty understanding and utiliz-
ing the Tao process.

70:2   The author of this work is trying to explain the Tao process and to show how to
utilize it. But, to people caught up in external superficialities, the Tao process is murky
and confused. The mystic sage seems alien, a sojourner from a distant land. The sage
has great value to the few who do understand. They know that under a coarse exterior
the sage carries a precious jewel.

For Thought:
So many people these days are out to save you and the world from their own particular
monsters. They intend to do this with or without your cooperation. This is a sign of the
times. These people are afraid to confront their own uncertainty, so they seek to con-
vince others of things that they don't really believe themselves. All people carry the ultimate truth inside them. What they have to do is to turn inward to find it.

For Action:
By now you probably have read most if not all of the Tao Te Ching. Scan through the
work and find a section or chapter that has particular relevance or appeal to you.
Commit to memory the part which you have chosen. Make the words come to life by carrying them in your heart. Visit there and look at your precious jewel whenever you feel
the need.

Related Reading:
Section 70:1   Read 53:1, 78:1
Section 70:2   Read 20:3

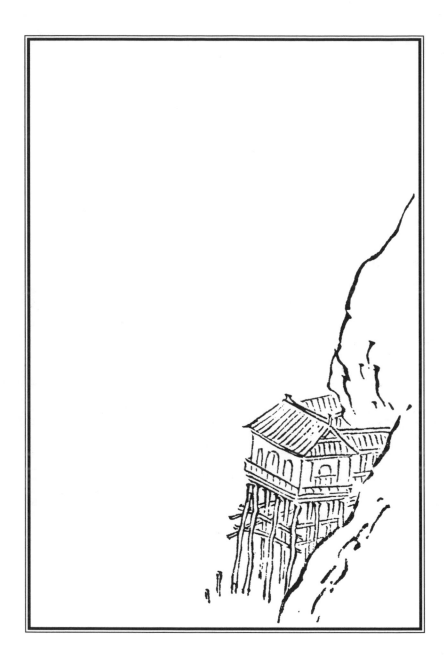

KNOWING NOT-KNOWING

71:1   To know you do not know is best.
        Not to know you do not know is a defect.
        To recognize a defect is to be not defective.
        Because he recognizes a defect,
        The sage is not defective.

Paraphrase:
71:1   It is better to recognize your own ignorance than to delude yourself.
Recognizing ignorance is the beginning of wisdom.

For Thought:
What some regard as knowledge may be ignorance. Erudition does not necessarily imply wisdom. So, one who is willing to recognize the insufficiency of pure book learning knows that he or she does not know. One does not really have a true grasp of any intellectual discipline until he or she internalizes it. Thus, in the true sage, even quantitative, linear, logical knowledge acquires a strong subconcious element which may appear to be an almost mystical intuition to an observer.

For Action:
Read Ezekial 2:8 - 3:1. Write down what you think it means.

Related Reading:
Section 71:1   Read 19:1, 48:1, 56 (all)

SELF-RESPECT, LOW PROFILE

72:1   When people defy authority,
        Even greater authority descends on them.

72:2   Do not cramp their space,
        Do not meddle in their livlihood.
        If you do not oppress them,
        They will not reject you.

72:3   Therefore the sage knows himself, but does not show himself.
        He respects himself, but does not exalt himself.
        Therefore he takes the one and discards the other.

Paraphrase:
72:1   Resistance to authority brings reaction by authority.

72:2   As a leader you will establish yourself more firmly by non-interference, than by meddling and oppression.

72:3   Know yourself without trumpeting your knowledge. Have self-respect, but maintain a low profile. Dwell on the inner person and discard the superficialities of the external world.

For Thought:
This chapter explores the results of oppressive leadership and defiant resistance. I am reminded of the events in Tienamen Square a few years ago. The defiant resistance put up by the students brought guns and tanks in response. From the other side, if there had not been oppression by the government, there would not have been rejection of authority by the students.

For Action:
We are conditioned to evaluate our own worth and that of others by the importance of our titles. For example, I am Distillery Operations Manager for the company for which I work. But it is not the title that is important, it is the constructive work which I do. Next time you are in a group of people where introductions are being made, listen to the titles. Think about the name attached to your own job and what you really do. Watch the surprise on people's faces when you introduce yourself by function instead of by title. When I'm asked what I do, I don't say that I am Distillery Operations Manager. Instead I say, I make whiskey.

Related Reading:
Section 72:1   Read 57:2, 74:1
Section 72:2   Read 58:1, 66 (all)
Section 72:3   Read 12:2, 22:2, 24 (all), 58:3, 77:2

FOLLOWING THE COURSE OF TAO

73:1   One with courage and daring will be killed.
        One with courage and gentleness will survive.
        One yields benefit, the other yields harm.

73:2   Heaven hates some things,
        No one knows why.

73:3   The Tao of heaven does not contend, yet is victorious,
        Does not speak, yet responds,
        Is not summoned, yet comes on its own,
        Does not act agitated, yet lays plans.
        Heaven's net is vastly vast.
        Its meshes are coarse, but nothing slips through.

Paraphrase:
73:1   The value of inner strength and resolution lies in its mode of application.
Bravado causes injury. Gentle yielding achieves victory.

73:2   The Tao process is difficult to understand.

73:3   The Tao process continues interminably without struggle. It responds naturally to each situation without being invoked. It follows its natural plan which includes
everything without exception.

For Thought:
Section 73:3 is an illustration of natural process which goes on all the time. Tao acts
without deeds, cannot be summoned or directed, and cannot be diverted from its
course. It flows like a deep river.

For Action:
Is there something in your life which has become a contentious issue? Think about what
is actually going on, not in terms of events, but in terms of underlying process. When
you have considered how and why the issue arose, decide how you can resolve it without going against the flow of the underlying process. Act on your decision and evaluate
the outcome.

Related Reading:
Section 73:1   Read 67:2, 69 (all), 30:1, 68 (all)
Section 73:2   Read 30:2
Section 73:3   Read 34:1, 37 (all)

THE PARADOX OF PUNISHMENT

74:1   If people no longer fear death,
Then why try to frighten them with death?
If they do fear death and we execute those who do not conform to the law,
Who would dare to be a criminal?

74:2   If people fear death, then there is a master executioner.
If we usurp the master executioner and kill for him,
It is as if we try to cut wood like a master carpenter.
If we try to cut wood like a master carpenter,
We will seldom fail to cut our own hands.

Paraphrase:
74:1   If people are not afraid of death, then there is no use in trying to frighten them with death. If they do fear death, then they will be deterred by the threat of execution.

74:2   If people fear death, then there is a master executioner. If any one of us assumes the role of the master executioner, then we will hurt ourselves like an inexperienced person cutting wood with a razor-sharp axe.

For Thought:
If one is not afraid of punishment, then punishment fails to teach or deter. On the other hand, if one is afraid of punishment, then it will teach or deter. There is no easy answer. Even further, if there is punishment, who will administer it? The old cliche which says of punishment, this will hurt me more than it hurts you, is true. If we become judge and executioner, how will we be affected by the responsibility for and consequences of our actions? That is the paradox of punishment.

For Action:
At work have you ever assigned a task to a subordinate with the idea of punishment or getting even? Think carefully and you will almost certainly come up with at least one situation where this occurred. What was the outcome of this situation? Did you or your subordinate learn anything? Was there animosity or tension between you and the other party? Did open warfare flare up as a result of your scheme to get even? How much better would it be to direct your passion at the process instead of people? Next time this type of situation arises work with your subordinate to identify and correct the problem rather than devising punishment for failures.

Related Reading:
Section 74:1   Read 57:2, 75:3
Section 74:2   Read 30:1

GREEDY LEADERS, IMPOVERISHED PEOPLE

75:1   People are hungry.
        It is because the government taxes too much,
        That the people are hungry.

75:2   People cannot be governed.
        It is because the government meddles too much in affairs,
        That the people cannot be governed.

75:3   People are indifferent to death.
        It is because they must strive mightily to live,
        That they are indifferent to death.

75:4   Thus those who do not seek constantly after life,
        Are superior to those who value life.

Paraphrase:
75:1   People are hungry for more because their leaders take too much.

75:2   People are rebellious and mean-spirited because their leaders constantly meddle in their affairs and tamper with their lives.

75:3   Some people are indifferent to death because their lives are so impoverished.

75:4   Those who do not seek constantly after the material
aspects of life are superior to those who constantly grasp for more.

For Thought:
This morning the front page of the newspaper carried three stories which relate to this
chapter. The first told of members of Congress who are retiring rather than running for
reelection. Many of them are quitting rather than face an electorate outraged by their
shameless use of perks and priviliges which are paid for by tax money. The second story
was about an FBI investigation of state legislators who alledgedly sold their votes and
influence to lobbyists for trips, vacations, and campaign contributions. The third related
the story of a local high school principal who violated school board policy by using public
funds to build a private bath for her office. She used a shop instructor to do the construc-
tion while a security guard was left in charge of the instructor's class. She also misused
and misdirected money from concessions and gym rentals which should have gone into
school accounts. Does power at any level corrupt? Does greed for material things drive us
all? Pogo the Possum said, "We has met the enemy and he is us." Was he right?

For Action:
When there is grasping and greed there is to the exact same degree impoverishment and
need. Do you agree? Also, the smallest oppression, if tolerated and condoned, grows. Do
you agree? If so, consider your day-to-day activities, especially at work. Do you take small
gifts from suppliers of goods and services? If so, does that place you under obligation to
the giver or affect your decisions about purchase of goods and services? What do the gifts
add to the cost of the goods and services which you buy? Do you have unecessary perks
associated with your job? Are the perks which are personally acceptable to you the same
perks which you despise when discovered fullblown in the hands of the powerful?

Related Reading:
Section 75:1   Read 53:2
Section 75:2   Read 65 (all)
Section 75:4   Read 50:1   155

THE WAY OF THE GREEN STICK

76:1   At birth, a man is weak and flexible.
        At death, he is hard and rigid.
        All living things such as grass and trees,
        Are supple and yielding while alive,
        And withered and dry when they die.
        Thus unyielding rigidity is the companion of death,
        And yielding flexibility is the companion of life.

76:2   Therefore an inflexible army will lose,
        The most rigid tree will snap.
        The hard and unyielding are lowered,
        While the soft and supple are elevated.

Paraphrase:
76:1   When we are young, we are flexible. When we are old, we are stiff. It is the
same in all of nature. Living plants are supple and green, full of sap. Dead plants are
withered, dry, and brittle. This lesson from nature teaches us that inflexibility leads to
loss and yielding leads to gain.

76:2   The strongest army will fall because it is tied to inflexible, unchanging tatics
and strategy by its size and strength. The tallest, strongest tree is the one most likely to
be blown over by wind or felled by axe. That which is inflexible falls, while that which is
supple is uplifted.

For Thought:
Taoism almost certainly has its roots much further back in antiquity than the time when
the Tao Te Ching was written or compiled. This chapter, with its references to the great
cycle of birth and death and to lessons drawn from plants, may show vestiges of an early
Neolithic or even Paleolithic matriarchate religion which emphasized the Earth Mother
and the feminine principle.

For Action:
Write down examples of people, processes, or systems which you think of as rigid,
unyielding, or orthodox and which have suffered as a result. One such example might be
the Communist system in Eastern Europe and the Soviet Union. Do the same for people, processes, or systems which you see as flexible and dynamic. Think about yourself
in the context of this chapter. Think of softness and suppleness as humility and open-
mindedness. Think of hardness and rigidity as arrogance and pride. How can you cultivate the former pair and eliminate the latter?

Related Reading:
Section 76:1   Read 22:1, 50 (all), 72:1, 78:1
Section 76:2   Read 30:2, 39:2, 40:1, 42:4, 43:1, 52:3, 61 (all), 77:1

EXCESS AND INSUFFICIENCY

77:1   The Tao of heaven is like stretching a bow.
       The top is lowered,
       The bottom is raised.
       The excessive is reduced,
       The insufficient is increased.
       Therefore the Tao of heaven reduces the excessive,
       And increases the insufficient.
       The Tao of man reduces the insufficient,
       And increases the excessive.
       Who, then, will give his excess to the world?
       Only the man of Tao.

77:2   Therefore the sage:
       Works without expectation,
       Accomplishes without taking credit,
       And does not wish to display his superiority.

Paraphrase:
77:1   The Tao process works like a bow bending. The maximum potentiality is achieved when the top is pulled down and the bottom is pulled up. The Tao process works the same way by reducing excess and increasing insufficiency. The way of man is exactly opposite in that more and more is taken from impoverished people and things to be transferred to those already in a state of superabundance. Only the sage gives away his or her excess.

77:2   Therefore the sage works only to expedite process, giving no thought to rewards or noteriety. The sage does not wish to display superiority.

For Thought:
There is a humorous saying which goes, those of you who think you know everything are irritating to those of us who do. That goes to the heart of many transactions and interactions which occur between people in today's world. Each person assumes that he or she knows more than the other and acts accordingly. The result is a deadly serious rough and tumble game of king-of-the-hill with jobs, careers, and sometimes lives, hanging in the balance. The fundamental question is whether we could all be more successful by expediting process, rather than dragging each other down.

For Action:
Think about your work and your interactions with your coworkers. Do you think that you know better than they, what needs to be done? Really evaluate the reasons for your feelings. How much is expertise and how much is ego? It may be true that you are more knowledgeable about process than others. If it is, practice helping people to understand your position, rather than simply ramrodding it through both peers and subordinates. Remember that the Tao process constantly moves toward equilibrium. If you push the equilibrium in one direction, it will react and push in the opposite direction.

Related Reading:
Section 77:1   Read 22:1, 76:2
Section 77:2   Read 2:2, 10:2, 34:1, 51:2

YIELDING OVERCOMES INFLEXIBILITY 78.

78:1   There is nothing in the world softer or weaker than water.
        Yet there is nothing better for wearing away the hard and unflexible.
        It cannot be replaced.
        The soft overcomes the hard.
        The weak overcomes the strong.
        Everyone knows this, but few put it to practice.

78:2   Therefore the sage says:
        He who accepts the humiliation of the people,
        Deserves to be the leader of the state.
        He who accepts the calamities of the state,
        Deserves to lead the world.
        True words are often paradoxical.

Paraphrase:
78:1   Water, though it is soft, wears away stone. There is no replacement for water in this function. In general, yielding overcomes inflexibility. This is known by all but practiced by few.

78:2   The sage who accepts humiliation deserves to lead. The sage who accepts calamities and misfortune on behalf of the state deserves the mantle of leadership. As strange as it may seem this is the truth.
For Thought:

Water truly is remarkable in its properties. Other compounds with a similar molecular weight are gases at room temperature. Water, because of a cohesive force called hydrogen bonding, is a liquid. This one property allows us to exist as living organisms. Water is as close to a universal solvent as there is in nature. Thus it carries dissolved nutrients to plants. It ultimately wears away rocks by dissolving slightly soluble components. It also has the unique property of expanding when it freezes. Water which finds a crack or crevice in a boulder can freeze and break it as readily as a jack hammer. The Taoist sages intuitively recognized these amazing properties of water and tried to emulate them in their daily living.

For Action:
Today emulate water in your activities. Instead of attacking head on when you encounter resistance, dissolve resistance by looking for compatibilities. Instead of blasting away obstacles with dynamite, weather them away by seeking cracks and crevices which can be chipped away by freezing. Be willing to cleanse situations by washing away the dirtying effects of blame and recrimination. Accept these destructive aspects like water carrying away pollution. Cleanse yourself naturally like water trickling over rocks and evaporating in the sun to form white clouds and pure rain. Be water today and reap the benefits of Taoist wisdom.

Related Reading:
Section 78:1   Read 36:1, 43:1, 70:1, 76 (all)
Section 78:2   Read 7:2, 8:1, 13:2, 66:2, 81:1

QUARRELS, QUIBBLES, AND QUIETUDE 79.

79:1   When a bitter quarrel is settled,
        Some animosity will remain.
        How can this be good?

79:2   Therefore the sage accepts his obligations,
        And does not demand payment.
        The man of virtue fulfills the contract.
        The man without virtue quibbles over terms.

79:3   The Tao of heaven is impartial,
        It is always with the good man.

Paraphrase:
79:1   Settling a bitter quarrel tends to produce a winner and a loser. There will
always be a feeling of aggrievement and animosity on the part of the loser. This cannot
be good.

79:2   So the wise person accepts obligations and does not make demands. This person will fulfill the contract while the person of little potentiality quibbles over terms.

79:3   The Tao process always works through people of great potentiality.

For Thought:
Have you ever sensed an undefined wrongness in a relationship or interaction with
someone? Such wrongness has a way of growing into tension. Tension grows into conflict and bitter quarrels result.

For Action:
Section 63:3 tells us to deal with things while they are small. In your interactions with
people be ultra-sensitive to your intuitive feelings of wrongness. When you sense
wrongness, address it with the person involved. It may be easier to deal with a small
bump of wrongness than with a barrier of tension or the blockade of a bitter quarrel. If
you find yourself about to utter harsh words or to quarrel with someone, stop. Think
about this chapter and the consequences it predicts for quarrels, even those which are
nominally settled.

Related Reading:
Section 79:1   Read 8:3, 66:4, 68:1, 73:3
Section 79:2   Read 63:2, 77:2

RUSTIC UTOPIA

80:1   The ideal community is small in size and population.
Though there is an abundance of tools,
People do not use them.
They regard death gravely and do not think of moving away.
Though there are ships and vehicles,
People do not ride in them.
Though there are armor and weapons,
People do not display them.
Records are kept by knotting ropes.
The people enjoy their food and dress in beautiful clothing.
They are contented with their customs and comfortable in their homes.
Though the neighboring village is in sight,
And the crowing of roosters and barking of dogs is heard,
The people are content to die at home,
Without ever visiting one another.

Paraphrase:
80:1   A small community is best. The people do not use tools because it is better and more fulfilling to work with the hands. They regard death gravely because life in the rustic utopia is good. They would not think of moving away. There is no need for transportation since no one wants to leave the small community. There is no need for weapons because people are at peace. They are content with simple means and happy with the basics. Though there are other communities nearby they do not visit them. They are happy to live and die where they are.

For Thought:
Upon reading this chapter you might recoil from the rustic, even primitive, situation described. But if you could shed your wordly sophistication and join these people in their simple contentment and serenity, would you do so? Is there not a touch of sadness inside you for your loss of innocence?

For Action:
A Zen master was once asked to describe his religious experience. He said, "I chop wood, I carry water." How different this is from the sentiment expressed on a bumper sticker which says, "A bad day at the lake is better than a good day at work." In your work tomorrow, whether at home or at the office, stop to consider what you have completed. How will your good job positively affect the next person to utilize your handiwork? Take a moment to rejoice in having work to do and the capability to do it. Your completed task is a manifestation of your potential. Remember, the work that you do can be a curse or a blessing. It is all up to you.

Related Reading:
Section 80:1   Read 12 (all), 31 (all), 36:2

165

TRUTHFUL WORDS

81:1   Truthful words are not beautiful,
        Beautiful words are not true.
        The wise man is not learned,
        The learned man is not wise.
        The good are not many,
        The many are not good.

81:2   The sage does not accumulate things.
        The more he does for others, the more he has.
        The more he gives to others, the more he receives.

81:3   The Tao of heaven to benefit without doing harm.
        The Tao of the sage is to act without contending.

Paraphrase:
81:1   Making speech flowery does not make its content true. Erudition is not wisdom. Very few are naturally good. Most are removed from their original nature.

81:2   Sages do not gather up to themselves. They give themselves to others and, in losing themselves, receive much in return.

81:3   The Tao process does no harm in its action. Taoist sages, likewise, achieve but do not argue.

For Thought:
Beautiful words may describe something, but when the description is done your rational mind only possesses a neuro-construct of the thing. You may have acquired knowledge of form, but you will have no understanding of function. Thus the learned are not wise. When we want to see form, we cast the sunlight of rationality on it. When we want to understand function and its connection to Tao process, we look at the stars and contemplate the cosmic Tao.

For Action:
You are at the end of the beginning. Read the Tao Te Ching again and again. Write down your own thoughts. Make up your own exercises for action. Get as many translations as you can and read them. Each time you approach the Tao Te Ching you will move further back down the path. You will find more and more subtle enlightenment. Drink the water of Tao and you will never thirst.

Related Reading:
Section 81:1   Read 48:1
Section 81:2   Read 77:1
Section 81:3   Read 8:3, 22:2, 66:4, 68:1, 77:2

APPENDIX 1: TRANSLATIONS AND INTERPRETATIONS

The following list is arranged chronologically to facilitate study of the influence that one translator might have had on another. It consists only of those translations and interpretations used in this work. In some cases, such as those of Waley and Wilhelm, it is difficult to determine when the particular edition actually first appeared. In these cases I have dated the translation as the earliest of which I am aware.

1891   Legge, James, translator. The Texts of Taoism. Part I. New York: Dover Publications, Inc., 1962.

1905   Medhurst, C. Spurgeon, translator. The Tao-Teh-King: Sayings of Lao Tzu. Wheaton, Illinois: The Theosophical Publishing House, 1972.

1910   Wilhelm, Richard, translator. Tao Te Ching: The Book of Meaning and Life. Translated from the German by H. G. Ostwald. London: Arkana, 1985.

1913   Suzuki, D. T. & Carus, Paul. The Canon on Reason and Virtue. La Salle, Illinois: Open Court Publishing Company, 1974.

1922   Mears, Isabella, translator. Tao Teh King. London: Theosophical Publishing House, Ltd., 1983.

1926   MacKintosh, Charles H., translator. Tao of Lao Tsze. Wheaton, Illinois: The Theosophical Publishing House, 1986.

1934   Waley, Arthur, translator. The Way and Its Power: A Study of the Tao Te Ching and Its Place in Chinese Thought. New York: Grove Press, Inc., 1958.

1944   Bynner, Witter, translator. The Way of Life According to Laotzu. New York: Perigree Books, 1972.

1948   Lin Yutang, translator. The Wisdom of Laotse. New York: Random House, 1948.

1955   Blakney, R. B., translator. The Way of Life: Lao Tzu. New York: New American Library, 1983.

1958   Bahm, Archie J.. Tao Teh King. New York: Frederick Ungar Publishing Company, 1958.

1959   Ch'u, Ta-Kao, translator. Tao Te Ching. London: Unwin Paperbacks, 1985.

1961   Wu, John C. H., translator. Lao Tzu: Tao Teh Ching. Boston: Shambhala Publications, Inc., 1989.

1962   MacHovec, Frank J., translator. The Book Of Tao. Mount Vernon, New York: The Peter Pauper Press, 1962.

1963   Chan, Wing-Tsit, translator. A Source Book In Chinese Philosophy. Princeton: Princeton University Press, 1963.

1963   Lau, D. C., translator. Lao Tzu: Tao Te Ching. New York: Penguin Books, 1963.

1972   Feng, Gia-Fu and Jane English, translators. Lao Tsu: Tao Te Ching. New York: Vintage Books, 1972.

1977   Lin, Paul J., translator. A Translation of Lao Tzu's Tao Te Ching and Wang Pi's Commentary. Ann Arbor: Center for Chinese Studies, The University of Michigan, 1977.

1979   Ni, Hua-Ching, translator. The Complete Works of Lao Tzu. Malibu, California: The Shrine of the Eternal Breath of Tao, 1979.

1981   Cheng, Man-Jan, translated from the Chinese by Tam C. Gibbs. Lao-Tzu: "My words are very easy to understand.". Richmond, California: North Atlantic Books, 1981.

1982   Maurer, Herrymon, translator. The Way of the Ways. New York: Schocken Books, 1982.

1982   McCarroll, Tolbert, translator. Recorded by Audio Literature, Inc., read by John Needleman. The Tao Te Ching. South San Francisco, California: Audio Literature, Inc., 1987.

1982   Wei, Henry, translator. The Guiding Light of Lao Tzu. Wheaton, Illinois: The Theosophical Publishing House, 1982.

1983   Tao Te Ching: The Book of Perfectibility. New York: Concord Grove Press,1983.

1985   Heider, John. The Tao of Leadership. New York: Bantam Books, 1985.

1986   Wing, R. L., translator. The Tao of Power. Garden City, New York: Doubleday & Company, Inc., 1986.

1987   Hwang, Shi Fu, translator. Tao Teh Chin. Austin, Texas: Taoism Publisher1991.

1988   Mitchell, Stephen. Tao Te Ching. New York: Harper & Row, Publishers, 1988.

1989   Chen, Ellen M., translator. The Tao Te Ching: A New Translation with Commentary. New York: Paragon House, 1989

1989   Grigg, Ray. The Tao of Being. Atlanta, Georgia: Humanics New Age, 1989.

1989   Henricks, Robert G., translator. Lao-Tzu: Te-Tao Ching. New York: Ballantine Books, 1989.

1990   Mair, Victor H., translator. Tao Te Ching: The Classic Book of Integrity and the Way. New York: Bantam Books, 1990.

1991   Cleary, Thomas, translator. The Essential Tao. San Francisco, California: Harper SanFrancisco, 1991.

APPENDIX 2: REFERENCES AND RELATED READING

Blofeld, John. Taoism: The Road to Immortality. Boston: Shambhala, 1978.

Bolen, Jean Shinoda, M.D.. The Tao of Psychology: Synchronicity and the Self. San Francisco: Harper & Row, Publishers, 1979.

Capra, Fritjof. The Tao of Physics. New York: Bantam Books, 1977.

Carter, Robert. The Tao and Mother Goose. Wheaton, Illinois: The Theosophical Publishing House, 1988.

Chang Chung-yuan, Ph.D.. Creativity and Taoism: A Study of Chinese Philosophy, Art, and Poetry. New York: Harper & Row, Publishers, 1963.

Cleary, Thomas, translator. Awakening to the Tao by Liu I-Ming. Boston: Shambhala, 1988.

Cleary, Thomas, translator and editor. The Tao of Politics: Lessons of the Masters of Huainan. Boston: Shambhala, 1990.

Cleary, Thomas, translator. The Taoist I Ching. Boston: Shambhala, 1986.

Cooper, J. C.. Taoism: The Way of the Mystic. Wellingborough, Northamptonshire, England: The Aquarian Press, 1972.

Grigg, Ray. The Tao of Relationships: A Balancing of Man and Woman. New York: Bantam Books, 1989.

Hoff, Benjamin. The Tao of Pooh. New York: Penguin Books, 1982.

Kaltenmark, Max. Lao Tzu and Taoism. Stanford, California: Stanford University Press, 1969.

Powell, James N.. The Tao of Symbols. New York: William Morrow and Company, Inc., 1982.

Smith, D. Howard, compiler and translator. The Wisdom of the Taoists. New York: New Directions Publishing Corporation, 1980.

Suzuki, D. T. & Carus, Paul, translators. Treatise on Response & Retribution by Lao Tze. La Salle, Illinois: Open Court Publishing Company, 1973.

Watts, Alan. Cloud Hidden, Whereabouts Unknown. New York: Vintage Books, 1974.

Watts, Alan. The Book: On the Taboo Against Khowing Who You Are. New York: Vintage Books, 1972.

Watts, Alan. Tao: The Watercourse Way. New York: Pantheon Books, 1975.

Welch, Holmes. Taoism: The Parting of the Way. Boston: Beacon Press, 1957.

Wilhelm, Richard, translator. The Secret of the Golden Flower. New York: Harcourt Brace Jovanovich, Publishers, 1962.

Related Reading:

Campbell, Joseph. The Masks of God (Four volume series). New York: Penguin Books, 1976.

Gooch, Stan. Cities of Dreams. London, England: Rider & Co., Ltd., 1989.

Smith, Huston, The Religions of Man. New York: Harper & Row, Publishers, 1965.